POVERTY

Human Consciousness and the Amnesia of Development

Rajni Kothari

Zed Books Ltd
London and New Jersey

Books by Rajni Kothari

Politics in India
Caste in Indian Politics
Footsteps into the Future: Diagnosis of the Present World and a Design for an Alternative
State and Nation Building: A Third World Perspective (Editor)
Democratic Polity and Social Change in India: Crisis and Opportunities
Disarmament, Development and World Order (Edited with Giri Deshingkar)
State Against Democracy: In Search of Humane Governance
Transformation and Survival: In Search of a Humane World Order
Rethinking Development: In Search of Humane Alternatives
Politics and the People: In Search of a Humane India
Towards a Liberating Peace
Growing Amnesia: An Essay on Poverty and Human Consciousness

This book was first published in South Asia, under the title *Growing Amnesia*, in the VIKING imprint by Penguin Books India (P) Ltd, in 1993.
Poverty was first published in the rest of the world by Zed Books Ltd, 7 Cynthia Street, London N1 9JF, UK, and 165 First Avenue, Atlantic Highlands, New Jersey 07716, USA, in 1995.

Cover designed by Andrew Corbett.
Typeset in Times Roman by Digital Technologies and Printing Solutions, New Delhi, India.
Printed and bound in the United Kingdom by Biddles Ltd, Guildford and King's Lynn.

ISBN 1 85649 339 3 Cased
ISBN 1 85649 340 7 Limp

For
Baba Amte, Mother Teresa,
Justice Krishna Iyer, Dalai Lama—
Lamp posts of conscience
in a world engulfed by a moral vacuum

Contents

Preface

In this essay, I have offered no theoretical framework, unlike in most of my earlier books. I have come to a stage in life, as well as in my intellectual journey, when I have given up thinking that theory can explain reality. Or be a guide to action. What follows is no more than a personal statement, a long argument as it were, on a matter that I consider to be very basic, yet one that the human community may already be turning its back on. If I have still used the conventional format of chapterization, it is only for the sake of convenience and some logical sequencing of themes. Otherwise, the same themes spill over from one to the other. The basic argument continues. And remains open even when the book formally comes to an end.

Also, unlike earlier, I do not intend to offer thanks to a long list of individuals and organizations. This is much more an individual product than a collective one: unlike my other books—except in the basic sense that my consciousness itself has been a product of a collective intellectual and political process. The key elements in this essay have been drawn from my own recent strivings—the theme of the growing exclusion and dispensability of the poor in my five-volume work on creating a humane world, my 'activist' involvement with the fate of diverse 'minorities' including the Dalits, the tribals and the backwards, my effort to push through elements of an alternative agenda when I was at the Planning Commission and my organizational endeavours through engagement in the Agenda for India, Lokayan, Independent Initiative, Federal Front and the Working Group on Alternative Strategies. For a long while now I have been concerned with the phenomena of 'two worlds' and 'two Indias'. This essay is a continuation of that concern. It is a concern that has deeply possessed me over the years.

I do want to thank Shekher Singh who has contributed in many ways—through discussions, draft notes, above all by holding firmly to his own views—to parts of this essay, and H.S. Chauhan who has worked closely with me through the several phases of this work, patiently and diligently producing drafts thereof. But while acknowledging such help, what is presented here is basically a personal exploration into a terrain that keeps eluding us all.

Rajni Kothari

Overview

In this book I want to deal with a subject on which I have not written directly or in a systematic way so far. The subject is poverty. Although I have written extensively on development (broadly from an 'alternative' perspective), as also on the condition of the poor and marginalized sections of our society and of the world at large, I have not written on poverty as such (except perhaps on the politics of poverty or on persisting states of systemic inequities, e.g., in my various writings on the phenomenon of 'Two Indias'). My only excuse for taking up poverty as an area of concern so late in my life, despite my knowing that it is a vast and complex subject, is that those who should be concerned about it are moving further away from either diagnosing and analysing the phenomenon of poverty and the new depths of destitution and untold human sufferings to which it has sunk, or providing new thresholds of understanding which can enable us to better deal with it and enable the poor themselves to overcome it.

It is not my intention to offer a criticism of economics or economists. The failure to extricate humanity from poverty and its pathological state at present is not primarily that of economists, for poverty is not basically an economic problem. Rather, it is a particular state of social, political, psychological and existential being that defines the human condition at a given point in history. Nor was the science of economics meant to handle the problem of poverty until recently when economic science became a so-called 'policy science', and a set of individual economists who came from a certain ideological background got concerned with the issue and its ramifications, as has happened with a number of leading Indian economists as well as foreigners working on India and other Third World countries. Further, what is called 'development' has not always been an effort to overcome poverty. At least in the Western industrialized countries (which most Third World élites would like to catch up with) development did not entail moving out of a state called poverty into one which we in this country are fond of calling 'poverty alleviation'. They simply entered a period of technological change, starting in the late eighteenth century, which in the course of time led to the phenomenon of industrialization that, over time, ushered in an era of progress and prosperity. (Incidentally, the original Theory of Progress that emerged from the European Enlightenment was not an economic concept.)

In short, economic development in the West consisted of a march towards affluence, a completely new development in human history which was first limited to the class that owned the means of production and then under *political* pressures from the labouring classes and intellectuals, and new political parties who took up their cause, spread to, larger sections of society. Poverty in these countries has been a phenomenon that grew as a result of affluence, and of internal crises and contradictions of capitalism as happened in the 1930s and as has started happening in recent decades, especially in the United States but also in other industrialized countries. The same is the case with poverty in the non-Western world which has been a consequence of capitalist development internationally and within each non-Western country. What seems to have happened is that human societies that adopted the path of capitalist development 'grew into poverty' and are now desperately trying to 'grow out'. (The capitalist dogma that it is through economic growth and higher rates thereof that poverty can be done away with, can be considered as part of such an attempt to 'grow out' of poverty.)

Poverty as a Consequence of 'Development'

The realization that poverty is a consequence of a certain model of development (and that the colonial outreach of world capitalism gave rise to structures where the new phenomenon of poverty was a necessary concomitant of the pursuit of wealth globally) had already emerged in the course of anti-colonial struggles and movements for liberation and national independence. In India it was clearly evident in Mahatma Gandhi's thought on both the causes of dependence externally and the causes of persisting poverty and large scale unemployment at home. And although Jawaharlal Nehru and the leadership of the Congress Socialist

Party were not averse to industrialization, they clearly saw the exploitative character of capitalism and the growth of poverty as a result of such exploitation. While there was a lot of difference of opinion between the Gandhian and the Nehruvian prescriptions for taking India out of the state of poverty brought on by colonial administration and dependent capitalism during the colonial period, they both agreed that poverty was the principal problem facing independent India. Poverty was seen as not just one among many problems which could be handed over to bureaucrats and technological experts on a departmental basis but something that pervaded all other issues and had thus to be the main focus of the new independent State. Political independence had to be translated into economic and social independence as without achieving the latter, the former was meaningless.

This perception was engraved in the constitution of independent India, particularly in the Directive Principles, in the setting up of the Planning Commission at almost the same time as the promulgation of the new republic, and Nehru's continuous emphasis on the theme of poverty and the need for a planned attack on it wherever he went during the course of his journeys covering the length and breadth of the country. The socialist leadership was even more insistent—in fact, far more than Nehru—on this basic condition in which the mass of people were to be found, namely one of acute poverty and suffering. It was Ram Manohar Lohia more than anyone else who shook the conscience of the till then upper class dominated Parliament by pointing out that the average Indian lived on ' 3 annas' per day and that the country—and the government of Mr Nehru—should be ashamed of this. And then of course there was the small but highly committed band of communists for whom the basic task facing the country was to bring down the inequity and injustice brought on by both the feudal and capitalist modes of production, and the need to frontally attack the causes of poverty.

Poverty as 'Structure'

Unfortunately, while all these streams of thinking understood that poverty was basically a political issue and had to do with the distribution of power in society, there was no clear thought given to building a distributive dimension into the institutional structure that was set up and evolved for the running of the State. Hence, while some attempts were made to take the country towards a measure of equality, e.g., through tenancy reforms and labour legislation and special provisions for historically deprived communities (the Scheduled Castes, Scheduled Tribes and backward classes), nothing was done to replace the colonial administration by a new structure of implementing the Directive Principles written into the Constitution or the 'socialist' thinking to which the Congress Party and the left parties were committed. In the course of time, the 'pragmatic' pull of vote-getting and financing the ruling party as well as the growing influence of landed and middle class interests in its organization, especially at the State level, and the disinclination to provide a clear ideological edge to the workers and the leaders in the party led gradually to handing over the policy process to bureaucrats and experts, with the party itself given a very minimal role in the running of the State. This failure to build an ideologically coherent party and instead the tendency to magnify the role of the government and bureaucracy in dealing with as crucial a task as removing the causes of poverty and eliminating the structures that perpetrated them, was to prove very costly in the decades to come.

In the process, planning itself became a bureaucratic and highly centralized operation, reducing states and districts to the mercy of the central bureaucracy. On the other hand, they allowed full play to the vested interests (business, industry, landowning classes, financial institutions) with the result that far from doing away with or at least reducing poverty and disparities, they were allowed to be accentuated. Not just in terms of widening gaps and growing inequities but also in terms of transforming the character of poverty from being a state of subsistence survival to being one of growing destitution and alienation from the very bases of survival, e.g., in terms of natural resources, community lifestyles and shared patterns of livelihood. And from being 'relative' to being 'absolute', and not simply in economic terms but in more total states of being. While the bureaucratic approach led to a fragmentation of the attack on poverty through a plethora of plan schemes, the basic structure of social and political power became more and more impervious to State intervention, with the result that while plan schemes and projects kept proliferating, resources and institutions and entry points to decision-making were increasingly cornered by small classes of people, mainly the urban educated middle class and the large landowning class, with little really percolating or 'trickling down' to large sections of the people.

As time went on, this situation got stabilized and institutionalized, with little scope left for correcting imbalances and reducing disparities, not to speak of undertaking any real structural transformation. In fact, one way of distinguishing the approach of the bureaucracy from that advocated by politically conscious people is that the former wanted to see poverty as a thing-in-itself, as a mere quantitative state of deprivation where providing a certain amount of income or food solved the problem. The latter, on the other hand, have seen it as an issue of equity and have, therefore, argued for structural changes. But such thinking has had little real impact, despite trying. Various governments have come and gone. Different parties have had access to formal power. Scores of committees and working groups have deliberated on major structural and programmatic issues. And, in the meanwhile, lots of warnings have been sounded by protest movements and growing social turmoil—between classes, castes and communities and between citizens and the guardians of the State—but all this without much impact on the real state of affairs. There has been no dearth of well-meaning leaders and even bureaucrats and experts. But they all seem powerless before the powerful forces (local, national and international) that have consolidated their position in the governance of the country. A manifestation of this helplessness was found in Rajiv Gandhi's admission that 85 per cent of the plan resources do not reach the people though of course he did not admit that this was largely a result of large-scale corruption, including among the political élite. And, later, in the decision by the next Congress government that succeeded him (after a short interregnum) to hand over the economy lock, stock and barrel to global institutions and foreign investors.

Poverty as Inevitable, Insoluble

The real and more basic manifestation of this state of helplessness is found in the tendency to underplay the very problem of poverty and act as if it did not exist. The new penchant for turning away from the past and forging ahead into the future, and joining the global march towards progress and affluence, also involves forgetting the poor and the oppressed, and the women and the aged. There is less concern for the coming generations and little sense of embarrassment or guilt (not to speak of anger and outrage) at the continuing exploitation and blatant violation of people's rights and dignities. Poverty is fast becoming a forgotten issue while describing the human condition. Key headlines in the media, the new slogans and the emerging prognoses put out by those in authority are no longer concerned with the basic condition in which a large part of humanity lives. It is a condition of absolute poverty with increases in states of ill-health, hunger and starvation. Furthermore, the goals of society and economy are no longer what they used to be; a considerable shift in the diagnosis of the reality facing us has taken place. This has gone so far that even ordinary people have been brainwashed into being hoodwinked by new desires and expectations—new consumer needs—that have been planted in their minds by the mass media and ad agencies. This in turn has resulted in deepening relative poverty as well. For the élite, neither absolute nor relative poverty is any longer a matter of primary concern for the State and for planned development. These are rather to be seen as unwanted and unpleasant realities to be wished away.

Even on the poverty front more attention is given to the social strife and violence that it creates and the law and order problems with which the élite has to deal. The long failure to face up to the basic malady of deepening poverty of both the absolute and the relative types has led the State, the élite, the bulk of the intelligentsia, the media and of course the whole civil administration and planning bodies to concentrate on symptoms that have arisen as a result of this basic neglect. In the meanwhile, misleading analysis of the key problems facing the country has detracted from the real issue, e.g., technological backwardness, fiscal crises, 'creditworthiness' abroad (credit with the masses no longer being an issue), queueing up for joining the world market and not being left behind, opening up the economy so that we become more efficient and competitive and so on. There has taken place a substitution of real issues with pseudo issues, real crises with pseudo crises as found in the current discussion of the economic crisis facing the country. Having failed to attend to the real structural parameters of poverty, we are now being made to accept the phoney ideas of 'structural adjustments' and 'structural reforms'. To refer to an issue raised earlier, we seem to have decided to move forward as a country towards affluence and to ignore the problems of poverty and pauperization in which the people of this same country are engulfed.

Era of Uncertainty

Underlying such a state of consciousness for which poverty is fast ceasing to be an issue lies a basic drift caused by loss of faith in the very vision and perspective that had sustained the earlier generation of nation-builders as well as the philosophy and outlook on the future that had informed such a vision. To this I will now turn.

Historically, we have entered a period of great uncertainty as regards both our understanding of issues and our approach to dealing with them. It is a period marked by a growing dissonance between our perception of reality and reality as it exists or is unfolding. Poverty exemplifies this in a most acute way.

Apart from this cognitive dissonance that envelopes all that we are engaged in—or are getting disengaged from—there are many other specific aspects of the environment in which we seem to be placed. Some of these are:

- Power struggles at the top that are fragmenting and tearing apart the 'system', the institutional fabric provided by the Constitution, and the moral framework we had inherited from the movement for national freedom;
- Deep-seated social turmoil, drawing in both traditional institutions like caste and ethnicity and modern structures of polity and economy, producing in its wake tremendous turbulence of a psycho-social type, growing schisms between communities, regions and identities and at the same time defeating all attempts at channelizing social energy along class conflicts with a historical dialectic informing them;
- The project of democratic nation-building with which we had started has been subjected to contrary pulls of centralized governance and the ideology of national unity at all costs on the one hand, and the growing demands of

pluralism, self-determination of each ethnic identity, human rights and competition for achieving equality for all on the other;

- A total lack of consensus on what we mean by justice and a just social order. It is the same with equity and in a different way, with the notion of diversity. And at the opposite end, with unity, totality, holism, integration, interdependence and other such notions of integration;
- Deeper still, the struggles against the inequitous State-sponsored model of development are themselves either getting fragmented politically and ideologically or getting marginalized or co-opted. Those who refuse to be co-opted and also refuse to be marginalized are brutally suppressed. 'Movements' as opposed to 'mainstream' are proving unable to hold, both getting pulverized by a new fundamentalism. 'Development' has also become a kind of fundamentalism.

New Fundamentalism

It is against such a background of drift and unresolved problems facing the State that yet another fundamentalism has raised its banner, namely that of the Market, backed by a new brand of 'élite populism' around the presumed promise and advocacy of the Market as an instrument that will end the monopoly of the State and make it easy for everyone. 'Liberalization' and 'privatization' are the other two catchwords that go along with the advocacy of the Market. With this the whole framework of issues and concerns that should inform economic development has drastically changed. Among other things, the whole rationale of development as a reduction of poverty and the promotion of equity goes. The whole focus shifts to deregulation, mainly for foreign investors and multinationals, though it is legitimized by promising a general era of deregulation domestically. We know that the latter has not happened except in the cases of a few powerful industrialists and contractors who in any case always had privileged access to the agents of the State. We also know that it will not happen for a long time to come, certainly not for the ordinary citizen or even the small entrepreneurs, given the structure of power and influence in our society. And yet, slowly and steadily, the view seems to be gaining ground that it was the State that stood in the way of progress and the prosperity of the nation and that such obstruction should be done away with. It is the Market that will ensure prosperity for the country though even the more strident propagators of the Market do not propose that it will remove poverty or even reduce its intensity. All that liberalization (based on the panacea of the Market) does is to 'open up' the country to outside influences. We should be clear in our minds that the 'opening up' ideology has little to do with the preservation or the enhancement of an 'open society' in which we have all along believed. The democratic movement over the last half-century has been struggling for this.

Liberalization should not be confused with liberty or liberation. When subject particularly to various conditionalities and pressures from global institutions, it can and probably will destabilize the democratic polity, put the masses under severe strain, turn against labour and further marginalize the poor. It will treat agriculture and the rural sector (especially rural industries and handicrafts) as arenas for exploitation. This is in addition to being deprived of the support that the State and the planning process had all along provided them with. Inherent in the new model of modernization and technology for which we are desperately seeking out multinational corporations will be a growing lumpenization of the traditional sectors that had provided both employment and security to millions of our people.

Erosion of the State

Perhaps the most serious outcome of the new economic thinking, both globally and nationally, is this undermining of the role of the State. This has been the main thrust of corporate capitalism and multinational corporations as the main carriers of the latest phase in capitalist development. While there is no doubt that too much dependence on the State had produced a structure of power and authority, at once insufficient and oppressive, as was indeed continuously pointed out by the left-cum-liberal critique of the State in Third World societies, today that very critique is being hijacked for a wholly opposite and right wing purpose by the proponents of globalization. Again, while the argument for liberalization has been gaining ground for a long time (in India it goes back to Rajaji's indictment of the license-permit Raj), it has of late become the basis for reinforcing privatization and debunking not just the public sector but the State as such, not just bureaucratic excesses but democratic politics itself, not just corruption in public life but the public arena as a whole.

The current thinking seems to be that, in the name of ensuring distributive justice, the State has inhibited 'production and growth' by suppressing the 'productive energies' of the Indian entrepreneur. That by removing controls this 'productive energy' will be unleashed and, combined with the levers exercised by the market forces, will ensure efficient, competitive production of goods and services. The State shall 'ensure' that the thus enhanced kitty is appropriately redistributed to help the weaker segments who may not *immediately* benefit from this economic upsurge. However, in time, if all goes well, everybody will start benefiting. Whatever that means.

But, of course, we also know that what has contributed to both the decline of the State as an instrument of equity and justice, of people's democratic rights, and the current right wing attack on it has been its failure to implement the radical measures that it had accepted in principle but all along failed to carry out. This ranges from land reforms to the 'right to work', from democratic decentralization to workers' participation, from employment guarantee to enabling the youth of the country to become the vanguards of a national renaissance. These and many other structural reforms have been continuously either simply ignored or deliberately sidelined by the ever expanding bureaucracy as well as the increasingly disoriented ranks of elected 'representatives'. While not falling prey to the new ideology of liberalization and the Market, we have also to take into account the limits of State action, given the strong vested interests that dominate the State. The key issue to ponder in the situation we face in India and elsewhere in the Third World is whether the State and the Market are the only two alternatives, given the fact that both of them are highly centralizing and élitist in their actual behaviour even if this may not be so in theory. In fact, are they really alternatives to each other? The Market can certainly not operate without State patronage. And, recent events in the former USSR seem to suggest that the State is also heavily dependent on the Market. We shall return to this issue later.

Changing Perception of Human Prospects

Underlying the present crisis in development are also some deeper and far-reaching changes in perceptions about human prospects and possibilities which we should be aware of if we are to come to grips with the crisis and evolve a realistic strategy to come out of it. For a long time, beginning with the nineteenth century, there existed considerable optimism about human prospects, covering the whole of humanity and for all generations. Building on the assumptions underlying the European Enlightenment, there developed an all encompassing Theory of Progress, in the main based on the promise of modern science and technology, positing an almost continuous growth towards human happiness. There also developed a full-scale philosophy of human happiness. The obstacles (e.g., institutional and historical) preventing the realization of it, it was asserted, could easily be removed both through State action and through the will of man. Hedonism was the term given to this philosophy. It ruled the roost during the Utilitarian phase of European, particularly British, liberalism.

In recent times the Theory of Progress has got translated into the paradigm of modernization according to which all societies could be modernized following the Western example, taken out of their traditional constraints, and liberated for an almost limitless enjoyment of the fruits of life. This was the outlook which influenced the modernist leadership of a large number of newly independent countries, alongside their attraction to industrialization and modern technology. This thinking also dominated the advice and expertise coming from the North in the form of intellectual models, aid-givers, professional economists and social scientists working in and outside the United Nations, international financial institutions like the World Bank as well as in national planning commissions and economic ministries. According to these thinkers, the only obstacle to realizing the full promise of technological modernization happened to be ideological (Marxism, nationalism and the hold of local cultures and traditions). Once these were pushed aside and the engine of modernization was given full scope, all the evils of non-Western societies (poverty, backwardness, unemployment, social disparities, even violence) would be removed.

This is no longer the ruling perception of human prospects. Apart from the alleged inadequacies and inefficiencies of governments and bureaucrats of the world and the growing evidence of diminishing returns of productive forces leading to a renewed sense of scarcity, there has also grown an argument over the last twenty years that there seem to be inherent limits to extending the fruits of modern science and technology, representing a reversal of the earlier optimistic perception of infinite growth under the regime of the modern development project. This position was forcefully stated in the publication, *Limits to Growth*, brought out by the Club of Rome in 1972. It was argued in this book that there are *ecological* limits to what humanity can achieve in terms of growth prospects, especially if it were to adopt the Western model of affluence and prosperity. It was pointed out then that the United States alone used up something like 40 per cent of the world's resources. If India alone were to achieve the American standard of living and consumer lifestyle, it will need much more than all the resources of the world. This particular outlook on human prospects was, of course, not allowed to go uncriticized. There developed a school of thought which argued that if human societies were to not follow luxurious standards for all and if the focus was on fulfilling the 'basic needs' of all human beings, the world still had enough resources to meet the needs of all.

Furthermore, as the debate became more widespread, it was pointed out by many, especially from the South, that the real issue was not resources but their availability to all. It was not as though there was a fixed and finite quantum of resources of various types but rather the growing inability of political systems to restrain patterns of consumption, especially of the upper and middle classes round the world, that had both led to current levels of industrial emissions and waste and produced serious imbalances between town and country, rich and poor and North and South. Given the present *structure* of world power and class interests, the *resources* too become maldistributed and thus increasingly unavailable for dealing with the problems of development. But of course, unable to stem the tide of élite consumerism, the élite itself feels a sense of the scarcity of resources. While this controversy has not to this day been settled, there have emerged many other compulsions, political, strategic and economic, arising out of the division of the world between North and South, East and West (a division that has by no means ended), élite and mass, which does not any longer permit the optimistic world-view that the modernization theory had once held out. Military expenditure alone takes away so much of the total resources of the globe. (It continues to do so despite the so-called end of the Cold War.) Prospects for economic assistance to developing countries which had at one time been loudly advertised under what was known as the Truman Doctrine have declined as there are many other demands to be met, particularly in the richer countries which are facing growing recession and unemployment and increasing states of social tension and ethnic convulsions, putting severe limits on what could be done for the poor and the needy not just in the Third World but all over the world. But, more than all this, there has emerged a new vision of organizing human enterprise, given the serious conflicts of interest between and within societies that have come to light, and which have produced new challenges like terrorism, social violence, extremes of the Marxist creed and, of course, more recently, the upsurge of ethnicity.

The emerging vision before the international community is no longer one of progress and prosperity but rather one of national and international security to be ensured by a conclave of global élites and the integration of effective markets round the world (in place of increasing 'effective demands' based on the rising purchasing power of the people and the enlargement of internal markets), and the growth of regional and global regimes of trade, technology transfers and investment. Underlining this decline in romanticism about the promise of modernity is an increasingly pessimistic outlook of what can be achieved through the sheer application of what is nowadays called 'political will'. Here the paradox is that at a time when, more than ever before, technological and managerial answers to human problems are in evidence, political élites are unwilling to use them, thanks largely due to the powerful nexus of interests (much beyond the military-industrial complex about which Dwight D. Eisenhower in his prophetic message to the American people had warned us all) that these élites have allowed to grow and dominate their lives as well as careers. It is because of this peculiar combination of emerging possibilities and a growing sense of helplessness all round that the outlook for the future appears so problematic. And it is out of such a changed outlook on human prospects that the chances of removing poverty and unemployment and disparities between and within societies seem to be receding. That, given such a combination of factors, we may have to live with these phenomena for decades to come is being felt and accepted by many. The increasing monopolies over resources and productive forces and the growth in exclusivist attitudes of the national élites have led to the gradual acceptance of the exemption of millions of poor, displaced, disenfranchised and powerless people. What has emerged out of all this is an as yet not fully spelt out doctrine of dispensability of those who cannot make it to either the corridors of governments or to the marketplace on which so much of the recent hope for development and progress is being placed. I shall return to the theme of dispensability later.

Emerging New Agendas

While such a striking reversal of concerns has been taking place in the whole approach to life and livelihood, to human welfare and human suffering, some other contemporary tendencies are making it difficult to revive interest on these key issues of human survival. We are witness to a number of new agendas that are drawing the attention of people and élites round the world and along which human energy is likely to flow as we move along the rest of the 1990s and 'march' into the twenty-first century.

Three kinds of upsurge are currently at work, each of which is likely to cause growing disintegration of the nation state as an institution and, in the process, push back concern over the condition of the poor and deprived sections of humanity. The first of these are the various democratic upsurges taking place round the world, presumably bringing down autocratic regimes and power structures—in the East, in the South and generally all over the world. Usually these upsurges are due to an urge to establish systems of government based on the liberal bourgeois model of representative democracy, often pursued by dissenting élites who are pitched against authoritarian regimes and are struggling to establish democratic governments in their place. The hope is being expressed that while such a shift towards democratic government will be limited to élites, ultimately it will benefit the people at large. The evidence available so far does not support such hope. We are aware of the enormous release of energy and excitement, first in Eastern Europe and then in the erstwhile Soviet Union, the long term consequences of which are yet to unfold. Just in a few months after the impact of 'glasnost' in that region there is evidence of growing frustration and disillusionment among the public that is giving rise to counter-demonstrations against the newly established 'democratic' leaders and regimes. There is as yet little hope that the historic assertion of the liberal democratic spirit in these and other countries and regions (Latin America, South-East Asia, Pakistan, Nepal and many other countries in almost all parts of the world) will in fact be realized.

Second, a series of ethnic upsurges are taking place alongside the liberal form of democratization. This represents an assertion of the cultural diversity and a growing search for identity and authenticity within existing nation states and beyond, in and across the boundaries that divide them from other nation states. Again, while one appreciates the search for a more plural and federal political order, it is not clear that the social and cultural expressions that it represents will necessarily address themselves to the basic condition of the people and their survival as both human beings and communities.

And then there is probably the most powerful upsurge of all, namely the upsurge of the Market and the strong appeal towards globalization ('integration into the world market') that is taking on diverse Third World élites as it did earlier with the erstwhile counter-élites in the socialist world. There is little hope that this marketization and globalization (and the underlying draw towards privatization of the economy) will 'trickle down' to the people at large and particularly the poor and discriminated sections of them, whether in the former socialist world or in the countries of the Third World. Instead, the existential condition of poverty, once it is steamrollered by the powerful impress of the Market, will degenerate into one of destitution, hunger and starvation and other multiple deprivations in access to livelihood and natural resources on which the poor had traditionally depended.

Perhaps the most serious set-back to achieving a more humane and just world and to removing the scourge of poverty and destitution has been the seduction of a large number of socialist countries by not just the capitalist model of development but also the consumerist model of the so-called 'free market', as well as by the dazzling technological 'miracles' of consumer societies. Not only is this halting the progress towards minimum welfare for all—a programme which was combined with a degree of austerity and distributive rigour (which unfortunately produced an unwholesome regime of controls and 'discipline')—it is also releasing levels of greed and exploitation that are affecting both social balances and the natural resource base of the social order. Globally, it is eating into the access to world resources and markets that are available to Third World societies, their erstwhile allies in the global power structure, 'betraying' the latter (if one can use that term) who had stood by them in their struggle against Western imperialism. And all this for 'catching up' with the West, not its democratic culture, but its model of development and consumerism.

All in all, we are moving into a period when development is being completely redefined and the already strong drive towards growing divisions between the rich and the poor everywhere—in the West, in the erstwhile East, in the South—will further deepen as the gains of the newly defined 'development' will be completely cornered by the few and millions will be excluded. This will be easy because the poor are not part of the Market—anywhere, including in the West—and also because they are perceived by the powerful and the prosperous as an embarrassment, best forgotten and allowed to 'stew in their own juice'.

Now, such an appraisal of the Market and of the globalist vision is not necessarily to accept or defend its counter, namely State-run enterprises or government programmes designed by planning bodies. The latter are known to have not delivered the fruits of development to the mass of people and are also known to be biased against the poor. They are also known to be amenable to the pressures of vested interests and politicians as a result of which the original intentions of such programmes are not carried out. State-sponsored development has also shown a tendency towards centralized, over-bureaucratic and insufficient and corrupt functioning. We also know that the State and its various agencies have increasingly become repressive and cruel *vis-à-vis* the poor and the radical movements that support the poor. All this is true. The problem is: Is the way out of this condition created by the centralized State, the Market, which will in all likelihood carry all the ills that there were in the State and add more of its own without providing whatever little spaces that are available in the State, its exposure to diverse pressures and its minimum norms of accountability especially in formally democratic societies like ours?

We should also recognize that the disenchantment with the State had taken place much earlier (ever since the mid-Seventies) when the attraction towards liberalization had started, and that therefore there is nothing terribly new about the current emphasis on liberalization, privatization and globalization. The processes of neo-colonialism have also been going on for quite some time. The point however is that all these processes of history are now being hastened at a pace and under an ideological construction that in fact amounts to a qualitative leap turning quantity into quality as Marx would have said. In fact, we already know enough about the destabilizing role of the introduction of the Market—in its new rarefied, consumerist, waste-inducing incarnation—into the real economy and into tribal and forest hinterlands, draining away resources and drawing away peoples and cultures from their diverse ethnic and ecological roots and steamrollering them all into a homogenized structure of goods and services.

The State itself played a role in promoting the entry of the Market into rural and social habitations but it was from time to time made aware of the inherent inequities and injustices that such a process had promoted and had often provided safeguards and correctives to exploitation and erosion of local communities that were involved in the very process of development from above. The same is the case with the role of modern technology and the imported model of industrialization which was subverting traditional lifestyles and knowledge systems. But again the same élites that controlled the State were persuaded to:

- Differentiate between different types of industrial development, in our case between large, medium, small and tiny sectors.

- Provide for minimum support and subsidies to the less powerful among them so that some kind of a 'balanced development' became possible.

Over time, of course, the power of the large sector has been growing and the interests of those living under the small and tiny sectors have been seriously affected, particularly after the rise of the technological model of development that emerged under Rajiv Gandhi. Within the framework of indigenous industrialization that had been pursued for more than four decades after independence was also an acceptance of the Market, the money economy and modern technology. But an essential part of that pursuit was a focus on poverty alleviation, reduction of unemployment and social disparities. There was also a slowly growing emphasis on the participation of the people through decentralized units at the district and lower levels. The unfortunate thing is that precisely at a time when a broad national consensus on the need for decentralization and people's participation and involvement in the decision-making processes is emerging, the new model of globalization based on the Market has been delivered to us as a panacea for all our problems. This historic turn around represents a complete reversal of the decentralized and democratic approach to development that had been articulated over time through a long process of debate and struggle.

Globalization

All this is happening under the global framework that has emerged in recent years, based on the vision of a 'new world order' being handed down to us by Uncle Sam from Washington D.C. The world-view underlying this new world order is that of creating and consolidating the whole of humanity under one common aegis, a shared philosophy and doctrine with designated roles for different power centres and regional alignments, an overarching technology and ways of distributing and transferring the same world-wide. The new audacity and arrogance with which such a world order has been promulgated has been possible due to a rapid sequence of developments, the most dramatic of which of course has been first the collapse of the Eastern European regimes and then of the Soviet Union, but no less critical being the gradual decline of élites and states of the Third World following their own inner failures at realizing alternative strategies of nation-building and then coming under the impact of the new model of globalization and integration into the world market. Also involved in the process of drawing Third World élites towards the globalist world-view has been the growing fear among these élites of internal movements of dissent and challenges to central authority, often taking highly militant forms, ranging from social militancy arising from class conflicts and struggles against economic exploitation to regional struggles for autonomy and self-determination to the growing political thrust of ethnic upsurges. All of these together are currently clubbed under the single rubric of 'terrorism'.

The diagnosis put forward by intellectuals and established interests in the West, but also widely shared among intellectuals and middle class interests in the Third World, is that all round the world there is emerging a threat from left wing forces which have also got aligned with Islamic and other fundamentalist forces, giving rise to a serious problem of preserving the security and survival of regimes and ruling élites. The threat is seen to be working both locally and regionally (cutting across state boundaries) as well as internationally. That the sources of such threats are themselves highly fragmented and lacking in a unified vision, that nearly all attempts at providing a truly eclectic framework while preserving cultural diversities—from Gandhi to the African dream—have failed is, of course, true. Hence the great vacuum created by what I have, in one of my recent writings, called 'a world without alternatives', a vacuum now being filled by the emerging global status quo based on a convergence of ruling élites.

Needless to say, the ground for such an emergence of a common interest among the ruling classes of the world had already been laid by, first, the defeat of socialism and, second, the waning confidence of Third World states in their capacity to provide an alternative vision of development and nation-building which was to 'de-link' from world capitalism and pursue its own independent and diverse paths that were sensitive to local conditions and the call of their distinctive cultures. It is this erosion of both the socialist and the Third World alternatives, both of which were to focus on the key issues of poverty, injustice and exploitation and were to produce alternative designs towards more humane and equitable societies, that lies behind the recent capitulation of élites round the world. The result is a much greater emphasis on issues of security and survival of ruling classes than on removing poverty, unemployment and disparities within and between societies.

The implications of accepting the 'new world order' should be fully understood. The role of the State in providing 'welfare' in the developed world and 'equity' in the developing world will slowly come to an end. The reason for this will be only partly financial (lack of adequate resources for social ends like education, health and housing). It will be more political as it falls prey to the model of privatization and globalization. It will also be moral based as it will be on denouncing the welfarist ideology and contempt for things like free health services or feeding the poor and the unemployed or even women and children in distress. There has already taken place a sharp decline in even conservative ideas of charity and compassion towards the needy and the poor as we move from a 'socialist' to a technocratic world based on hi-tech and integration into a single world market. Also gone will be the idea that the objective of economic development was a narrowing of disparities and a general lifting of standards of living and livelihood or, as was the jargon in India, lifting millions from below the poverty line. This is no longer a rationale of economic development. Development principally means raising of national averages ('per capita' incomes and wealth), catching up with the industrialized countries, the principal instrumentality of which has to be technology (mostly imported) and the key institutional means of which are to be the multinational corporations (MNCs) to which we are being implored to 'open up' as they alone, we are told, can bring in the latest know-how in technology and undertake the long overdue 'structural reforms' in the system.

In this perspective—which has already been accepted by most national élites—issues of poverty, inequity, disparity and unemployment are to be left out from the objectives of development. And this at a time when there has been a sharp decline in social justice and we are already facing a highly unjust social structure (both in its inherited and traditional forms and in the newly created ones). Indeed, the inequities have been getting worse, ever since the focus of development shifted from social goals to technological goals—the two need not be antagonistic but have been made so due to the impact of the new ideological package—and the prime instrument of development shifted from the State to the Market—these too need not be counterpoised against each other but have been as a result of our acceptance of the model of liberalization starting in the late Seventies and throughout the Eighties.

There are still other implications of accepting the new model to which reference has already been made earlier. The importance of the State will decline not only as a catalyst of development but also as an instrument for redressing grievances, providing correctives where injustices have occurred and processing demands of the deprived and the disinherited sections of society. Unfortunately, the new institutional model will lead to a decline in interest (till recently quite pronounced) in North-South disparities and consequent arguments for 'transfer' of resources as was argued, for instance, by the various independent commissions, from the Brandt Commission to the Brundtland Commission to the South-South Commission of which President Julius Nyerere was the Chairman and Dr Manmohan Singh was the Secretary-General. It was also the rationale of the various UN development decades, from the first to the second to the third.

Further, with globalization (as distinct from globalism espoused by radical thinkers from the West as well as the South) the trend towards decentralization of secular authority and decision-making will get reversed. Because, of necessity, the focus of effort will move away from the masses and towards the classes. The farther away the focus of thinking and deciding about 'development', the more excluded will become the peripheries, the size of which will keep growing and will in a short time include sections of the middle class as well. With globalization, political units of the federal and decentralized kinds will become distant. State-centred development was already becoming centralized under authoritarian regimes (including those that operated under formally democratic systems). Globalized development will be even more centralizing. And, with the monopolistic trend inherent in the model of the Market and of privatization, the quality and intensity of centralization can be imagined.

Implications for Culture and Ecology

Beyond the macro politico-economic implications of the globalizing framework that have been laid out above, there are several other aspects that call for our attention. First, there is likely to be an erosion and destabilization of indigenous cultures under the impact of the powerful thrust at homogenizing the world, a process that had already begun due to acceptance by the modern State of an exogenous model of modernization but which will now be given a much stronger and uninhibited push given the fact that the socio-political bulwarks that were available because of the relative autonomy of diverse nation states will become less and less so. The latter had played a mediating role in the confrontation between tradition and modernity, and thus between external and indigenous structures and values. Even though the latter will continue to exist and provide means of combating the universalizing and homogenizing consequences of a globalist world economy and polity, they are likely to be increasingly on the defensive. It is not that there is any special need to preserve each and every cultural landscape as it has always been. The real issue is how in their exposure to modern transnational culture and communications, they are not forced to 'adapt' so much as to lose their autonomy and their authenticity.

Indeed, perhaps the most corrosive, vulgar and demeaning impact of the new world order will lie in the area of communications. Standardized education and centralized information channels through which a worldwide 'mass society' could be fashioned will become the most pernicious instrument of creating such a society. Modern consumerism, permeating all societies through the mass media, ad agencies, Star TV and other such satellite technology, has already started straitjacketing desires and felt needs, exposing peoples and cultures to the global Market, upsetting the preferences and priorities of people (including unfortunately, the poor among them) and, above all, distorting production priorities themselves, manufacturing goods that have no relevance to people's needs. The defence mechanisms of traditional societies, their inherited knowledge systems and their ability to enjoy the fruits of nature in its immense diversity are thus being threatened.

But while such a process has already begun, there are still vast spaces of human culture and civilization, the large hinterlands of tribal societies, forest people and peasantry that have not yet gone under. Though aware of and occasionally influenced by passing fashions, these peoples have still maintained their individual and collective selves and are also, in many places, resisting encroachment by modern development projects such as high dams, thermal plants and nuclear installations. In most countries this conflict between imposed development projects and traditional cultures and habitats is going on and, whereas the bureaucratic power and financial resources behind these projects appear to have an upper hand, the struggles waged by local cultures and populations are also spreading, asserting their conviction about their own diverse world-views and their ability to fight for their own rights. The question is, what will be the balance between a centralized development process and decentralized community assertions under the new globalized version of modernization, the principal focus of which is to transform every individual into a consumer and every group or community (or nation for that matter) into a market? It is interesting in this connection to note that in the new drive towards integrating national economies into the world market through MNCs there is going to be a shift of emphasis from investment in capital goods and infrastructure to production of sophisticated consumer goods made for the élites and the new yuppie class through investments in things like food processing, packaging, marketing for urban and foreign markets, taking advantage of virtually bonded labour provided by these countries, including underpaid women and child labour, practices that are forbidden in the home countries.

The point is that the whole culture of industrialization and development that is on the anvil will have little to do with what has been traditionally associated with economic development and which in fact was what was attempted through State-sponsored development in which the public sector played a major role for providing the basic technological infrastructure. This is all now being given up in the name of privatization and liberalization, in the process giving a complete go-by to the redistributive demands of local populations and the poor among them. The 'Market' that will matter henceforth will be the one provided by the global middle classes and élite population whose main needs are no longer drawn from the need to industrialize the nation and create an infrastructure for long term development but on fulfilment of immediate desires and avarice ('greed' in Gandhi's terms). Hence the increasing accent on the service sector. It is not industrialization but agri-business and the expansion of the service sector (not to be confused with social services which will receive less and less budgetary support), mainly through banking, insurance, hi-tech education, sophisticated health services for the élites, mega projects of housing construction and transport meant for élitist uses, that we are going in for. Consumerism in the new era is to be not just in respect of marketing new goods and services but also in respect of pressing Third World economies into fulfilling the tertiary needs of a globalized consumer class, once again turning these economies into colonies. This used to be the case before national planning and development began. Now the latter is being discredited and delegitimized.

Second, there will be fairly massive destruction of the environment as a result of the penetration of multinationals and local corporate entities. The external interests that were obtained in countries like India, through foreign aid and transfer of technology, had ignored the rural sector which was thought too backward and too riddled with ignorance and superstitions. This was all to the good because it left rural and tribal societies free from external penetration. However, now, with the accent on consumerism and the revival of interest in turning rural hinterlands into colonies in which large tracts of land and forestry are to be drained for fulfilling metropolitan needs and desires, new technologies will be introduced to yield new produce—cash crops, social forestry type of plantations, food processing and packaging for the urban market. It is precisely the rural hinterland, including wastelands and dry farming zones, that is of interest to the new breed of MNCs. There will consequently be a much bigger onslaught on natural resources which the poor have depended on for so long for their survival. There has already been a decline in the protection that was traditionally provided by the State development agencies, and a series of legal enactments—because of these even as deforestation and desertification were on the increase, there was scope for appealing to the environmentally conscious sections of the ruling élite and sections in the government, as well as creating special cells and commissions for the protection of tribal communities, all of which made for a degree of accountability in the system.

All this is now likely to go under as the accent will be on producing for the Market, particularly the export market, and to this end, producing such items as have a chance to be exported, which increasingly means converting agricultural produce more and more to cash crops and other commodities which, even if needed at home, must be exported as the earning of more foreign exchange will take precedence over meeting home needs. The external debt to which countries like India are being subjected in the wake of their integration into the world market is increasing. Although a lot of foreign aid and even World Bank loans include clauses on environmental protection, all of them know, as does the government, that these stipulations can be violated in the same way as the Environmental Protection Act and environmental conditions insisted upon while clearing projects are violated without the batting of an eyelid. The long struggles over Narmada, Tehri, Suvarnalekha, Kaiga and Baliapal have increasingly brought out the particular doublespeak the government is indulging in, which is greatly influenced by business and contractor lobbies. With the new set-up that is in the process of being established, the Environment Ministry will be more and more marginalized. The various movements will face increasing repression and the long term ecological disasters that we all know are bound to follow will be knowingly ignored. If anything, the anti-environment lobby that is already growing will grow further as the integrationist view grows and with it the emphasis on 'export or perish'. The failure of environment activists to link ecological concerns with issues of economic security and survival of the masses is partly responsible for the appeal of the anti-environment lobby. All this, of course, entails something far more basic, namely the brainwashing of not just the opinion making élites under the impact of global influences but also of the people at large—at the altar of consumerism.

Third, and this follows from what has just been said, such a narrow and instant approach to consumerism will also entail using up productive resources and natural endowments here and now for immediate and at best medium term gratification with serious consequences for future generations. It used to be thought that development entailed laying the basis for better prospects for future generations and hence there was a need for restraining immediate demands for consumption and saving for a better future for the coming generations. There was something fundamentally Indian in such a view of life and limits on oneself which was reinforced by the early emphasis in development thinking in which savings and curbs on luxury consumption were an integral part. All this is already being given up with the growing demands of consumerism. In the coming decades this will get more pronounced because it will be a result of both consumerism at home promoted by globalized communications and the need for extorting more and more resources from the rural areas for fulfilling export obligations as part of 'integrating into the world market'. There is no room in this dual erosion of productive resources for caring for future generations. Even the poor are being pressurized to go for immediate gratification as well as to produce for the merciless market. For they too are in debt to their creditors—be it the moneylender or the banks—as is the country at large *vis-à-vis* its moneylenders, namely the World Bank/International Monetary Fund (IMF), the international commercial banks on which it is going to be more and more dependent, given the overall global strategy of forcing developing societies into the debt trap. With both the people and the state agencies perpetually in the grip of growing consumerism on the one hand and growing indebtedness on the other, where indeed will there be any scope left for future generations or even for the younger generation for whom the future holds little in store?

Political Implications

There are serious political consequences inherent in the emerging nexus between new institutional arrangements, new values and new individual drives through which people are being 'marketized'. Quite apart from the decline in the role of the State in preserving spaces for the underprivileged and protecting peoples and cultures from globalizing trends, there is the danger of the whole normative framework of democracy being undermined. The assumption that the liberalization of the economy would lead to a more liberal polity and generate more liberties for individuals and groups is thoroughly unfounded. On the contrary, it will reinforce the authoritarian tendencies of the ruling oligarchy which has already eroded the basic institutions of democracy and is making the State more and more repressive and vindictive towards the so-called 'weaker sections'. The institutions will be further eroded once whatever little welfare orientation there was in the Indian State is discarded or considerably reduced. Already one notices that several of the IMF/World Bank conditionalities are forcing the government towards anti-labour, anti-rural and anti-poor positions which may be to the liking of the business class or even the professional middle classes but will certainly not produce a more democratic ethos. Even in the West what has kept democracy going is not liberalization or privatization but, despite the ideological baggage, the continuing role of the State in protecting the poorer classes from the inequities and monopolistic tendencies of capitalism. That with the withdrawal of the welfare commitments of the State during the Eighties there was a rise in poverty and unemployment and even the pauperization of sections of the middle class, with serious social repercussions, was recognized by all. Hence the more recent trend in the West for restoring the welfare commitments of the State.

From this follows the whole question of the relevance of corporate capitalism in dealing with the serious crises facing diverse societies and nations. The edifice of liberalization and privatization at home and globalization abroad was announced during the Seventies—and earlier during the late nineteenth century—based on the assumption of the dynamic and progressive role of the capitalist system under which opportunities were to keep broadening and including all classes and regions of the world. This assumption proved unjustified. I have dealt with it earlier, while discussing the dramatic change in perception of human prospects that has already taken place. To that one should add that the Western economies themselves are in deep trouble. In particular, the United States which continues to be the dominant world power, but which faces serious problems at home following the sharp decline in the rate of growth, increase in unemployment, huge budget deficits and serious Balance of Payments (BoP) crises and is being forced to enact high-tariff walls against imports while at the same time coercing the governments of the developing countries to fall in line with its global trade regime through the General Agreement on Tariffs and Trade (GATT) and other international agencies. Even in the European Community, which is supposed to be better placed than the United States, there has been an increasing trend towards recession, a sharp decline in growth, and growing racism *vis-à-vis* migrants from the developing countries.

The frequent recurrence of recession in the West (which affects us too in terms of reducing our export prospects) reminds one of the Great Depression of the late Twenties and Thirties. What saved those economies and the capitalist system then was not F.A. Hayek with his radical advocacy of free markets, but J.M. Keynes with his advocacy of positive and large interventions in the Market by the State. The 'New Deal' in the United States, the rise of the Welfare State in Western Europe, and the distinctive Japanese model of social security and industrial relations lie behind the survival of democracy under capitalism. The effort made over the last decade to move away from this through Reaganism and Thatcherism, which looked like working for a while, brought in its own problems. Today both Reaganism and Thatcherism are dead and there is the renewed role of State-owned credit mechanisms for meeting with both economic and fiscal challenges. The pity is that neither this, nor the experience of the Latin American and African countries that had accepted the IMF/World Bank advocacy of free market, has been studied by our leaders. They have quite blindly gone in for an erosion of the role of the State, for an acceptance of the Market as the key mediator in the development process, and for globalization. In doing so they have walked into a trap laid by global hegemonic interests—not just a debt trap but also a trap for recolonizing large parts of the world (including the MNCs buying up capital assets and entire industries as has already happened in Latin America in the name of offsetting debt).

That all this has been a result of political exigency and the survival needs of a few leaders rather than of any clear ideological commitment only adds to one's dismay at the lengths to which ruling élites can go. Whether the result of ideological brainwashing or opportunistic politics, the brunt of the new policy package will be borne by the poor. Given the far-reaching amnesia about issues of poverty and survival, this is unlikely to affect the public conscience as used to be the case in days gone by. The transformation in the moral standards of the middle class needs to be taken note of in this context. For it was this class that was inspired by the national movement by Gandhi and by the vision of building a humane and progressive India. It was also the class that earlier carried the more traditional values of charity and compassion towards the poor. There was also an element of calculated rationality behind this generosity—if the poor could be helped out, educated and provided with minimal health and nutrition, they could be made to provide the type of labour necessary for productive purposes—the classic 'reproduction of labour' theory.

Politically too it was useful to carry the labouring classes along. What seems to have happened in recent times is that with an unprecedented expansion of the middle class itself and the growing importance of technology in place of labour, it has become politically feasible to explicitly exclude the poor from the social process.

Emerging Scenario

The overall scenario that is emerging is one of a growing divide in the human community—between and within nations, in the South in large measure but also in the North, between high consumption élite classes and the poor. This at a time when the State too is abdicating its responsibility by the weak and the vulnerable and handing things over to the Market which respects only those with money and 'purchasing power'. It is a situation that need not have arisen. The march of history was supposed to produce a more peaceful and prosperous and hence more united world. Even technology was supposed to help man achieve such a state. Unfortunately, the vulgar consumerist and self-centred, overly individualistic trend that modern industrial societies fell for has created the same seductive pull for the middle classes in the developing world. It lies behind the growing gaps and divides that inform the human community today, and a turning away from and a growing amnesia towards the poor everywhere. That this in turn will also render the global economy more rather than less vulnerable is not yet fully realized. That it will also generate new tensions and anomie in various societies is also not yet realized. In the North this is manifesting itself in growing revulsion against immigrants and 'refugees' who have been on the run following the massive destabilization caused by the rise of a new world order, while in the South the same attitudes are leading to not just a neglect of, but a growing sense of despair at, and contempt for, the poor. 'If only they did not exist'.

In all this, is there no sign of hope? Of course there is. Throughout history, whenever human prospects appeared dismal and bleak—the Great Depression, the rise of fascism and the Nazi onslaught, in our own land the long period of subjugation and slaughter of some of our bravest people by an arrogant foreign power—while it has produced depression and despair, it has also led to bold and creative responses that in the end successfully defeated what looked like an insurmountable problem. In our own time too we have been witness to a whole series of struggles against oppression and domination, external hegemony and internal exploitation. There are also signs of new alignments and new churnings of the human spirit against threats of the erosion of institutions and dignities. But alongside all this and giving further spur to it is a more basic dialectic of the very historical process that may appear to be linear and irreversible but cannot be so. It is a historical process that is already showing signs of considerable flux and drift, and is full of yawning contradictions. Already, the bullying methods employed by the US and US dominated agencies like the IMF, the World Bank and GATT are producing strong reactions. Even the 'pragmatists' among policy-makers are getting concerned at the amount to be sacrificed at the altar of the Market in return for the autonomy and stability of the State. Meanwhile, the very regions that looked as though they had 'collapsed' before the march of the MNCs—Russia, Eastern Europe, the Central Asian republics, China on the one hand and the stronger among the nations of the developing world on the other—are going to face domestic pressures and unforeseen consequences of the new development package as well as nationalist protest against the new *Pax Americana*, the 'new world order'. And as far as the poorer classes and the unemployed youth are concerned, the response will increasingly be more than one of mere discontent and disenchantment. It will express itself in two distinct but related ways. On the social and economic plane it will be increasingly class-based and violent while on the regional plane it will strengthen separatist forces and human rights movements among minority, tribal and nationality groupings. All this will happen when the 'new' hegemonic world order will become more and more unstable and unable to handle the wide array of countervailing tendencies. All the way from the 'revolt of the masses' to the declining enthusiasm for the new order among professional and ruling élites feeling insecure and entrapped in the global structure of financial dependency, squeezed between internal revolt and external commitments.

But with all this, the question will still remain: who will benefit out of all this turmoil and trauma—the professional mafias that thrive on conditions of alienation and anomie or the real underdogs of history, the poor in our case? To this there is no clear answer. It will depend to a very large extent on whether, alongside the convulsions in the secular sphere, there takes place a renewed emphasis on basic human values, a renewed capacity of human beings everywhere to get back to the essence of civilized being that can resolve the deep divide that at present characterizes the human condition. And it will depend on *politics*, on democratic politics, not just electoral politics but a politics based on critical interventions that will once again give a sense of hope and confidence to the poor and marginalized sections of society, generate a process of empowerment, a new realignment of forces and, out of it all, a new agenda for the State, in the process restoring to the State its role in democratic nation-building. Central to such politics and such an agenda will be the need to transform the nature of the State itself.

The Global Setting

In order to properly perceive the world setting in which developing countries like India and, in particular, the poorer sections of these countries are likely to be placed, it is necessary to understand the emerging structure of global power that will be established in the years to come.

Politically, with respect to the relations between states, there has taken place a dramatic change in the system of power relations that has prevailed almost since the end of the Second World War. What we had was at once a bipolar and tripolar world. It was a mistake to have described it as a bipolar world in which it was assumed that only the two super powers mattered and between themselves decided the fate of the world. It was no doubt predominantly bipolar in the military-strategic sphere and because of the dangers inherent in an increasingly escalating arms race, including the possibility of annihililation of the human race, attention was focused exclusively on the super power rivalry and, hence, domination of the world. But outside this militarized view of the world there existed a wider political structure based on both power relations and other issues on the agenda of the world which went far beyond the bipolar definition of 'world order'. The large majority of the states that constituted the world, among themselves representing the bulk of the human population, which may have been individually weak and vulnerable but which together could not be wished away, nor be co-opted in military alliances and security blocs, lay outside the bipolar definition of world affairs. Many of them also acted collectively—the non-aligned movement, the G-77, the Organisation of Petroleum Exporting Countries (OPEC) challenge to the world status quo and, following this challenge, the search for a New International Economic Order (NIEO).

More important was the very fact of a Third Pole and its claim to represent such a large part of human aspirations and to engage in the task of redefining the human agenda, which also produced a body of truly global public opinion in which citizens, intellectuals and activists from all parts of the world participated. In course of time (with the deepening of the global crisis) these latter engaged themselves in a variety of new social movements, and there was an upsurge of consciousness. Through all this the inherent instability of the bipolar military and strategic balance was held in check. What now appears to be coming to an end, then, is not just the balance and mutual deterrence provided by bipolarity but also the more dynamic initiatives and mediating roles for moving towards a more just and equitable and hence more stable and sustainable world order in which a larger arena of states and peoples was involved.

Institutionally too, there was the moderating role of the United Nations, moderating the results of the arms race and the race for global hegemony as between two competing ideologies but also over time providing for forums of opinion as well as action for the marginalized and the weak, the remaining vestiges of imperialism and, of course, the more basic human entities such as the children of the world, the women, the millions of refugees around the world, the tribals and indigenous peoples, the regional cultures and civilizations, above all the poor of the world in the service of whom such a large part of the United Nations network of institutions and the non-State and non-governmental network of institutions have been devoted. What made all this possible, institutionally and politically, economically and culturally, was the broad acceptance by the nations of the world of the 'development agenda'. Today, one faces the prospect of this going under as well. For, almost overnight, the United Nations has found itself reeling under the hegemonic clout of Western capitalist powers predominantly the United States. It may sound paradoxical, even ironic, that just at a time when the world was supposed to be moving towards increasing scales of disarmament and was becoming one in which military power was declining, the US was able to continue as the 'Number One' power of the world precisely because of its military preponderance and capacity to indulge in bloody adventures like the Gulf War. It may be the most indebted country of the world, facing a recession at home, in the grip of growing poverty, unemployment, lack of shelter and ordinary means of livelihood for millions of its people, as also facing the most serious racial and class wars in its history, and yet it manages to continue to be the 'Number One' that is able to call the shots and move round the world like a big bully and tyrant.

New *Realpolitik*

With the dramatic erosion of the socialist world and the near collapse of the Third World—as well as the *idea* of a Third World which would have offered a (third) alternative alongside the socialist alternative—there has emerged a wide vacuum, an unnerving and frightening vacuum that poses the prospect of returning to the 'law of the jungle', at least in the conduct of international affairs but perhaps also, as a consequence thereof, in the conduct of governments and vested interests domestically as well. The imposition of the market model and the ideology of privatization on such a de-institutionalized and disembodied structure of reality can well be imagined. But more on this shortly. For the moment it is enough to note that in the emerging vacuum that is likely to unfold in the coming years—vacuum both in the power structure of the world and in the institutional domain—the only recourse and stratagem left to governments and other centres of power will be that of *realpolitik*. And this time round (unlike in the long transition after the Napoleonic War and the Vienna Congress) it is going to be *realpolitik* without a framework of norms and conventions and an overriding liberal international set of values and limits. This will give rise to growing normlessness, insensibility to the human condition, and an increasing resort to bullying and to not just threats but, off and on, carrying out those threats so that no one dare challenge the omnipresence of a so-called 'unipolar' world order any more. (Logically, of course, there cannot be a unipolar world; polarity assumes more than one pole. But, then, we are fast moving into a world that will have neither logic nor rationality to it. What is more, the American dream has all along consisted of casting the whole world after its image, of constantly moving frontiers, of a dynamic integration and homogenization of the human race which can, under its aegis, be made a wonderful thing to live in.)

In the new *realpolitik* that is likely to be played out through its various combinations of actors and initiatives, different from earlier periods of instability and transition, there will be much more than the normal play of economic, financial and technological power. This is largely because the relative autonomy of both the states and the state system from the world corporate capitalist structure is fast coming to an end. So that, for instance, the role of diplomacy in the conduct of foreign relations, or of professionals working on the problems of poverty or of bridging the large gaps between societies and regions, is likely to be overshadowed by the logic of world capitalism and the need to integrate diverse economies and markets (including various social systems underlying production relations at different levels) into one large world market and global system of finance and management. Not only do we face a fast changing world scenario of power relations, we also face a fast changing nature of capitalism, both in the extent of its global reach and in its defining characteristics.

Role of Technology

First, the relations of production are going to be induced much more by technology, and hi-tech at that. In the past, too, technological changes mattered a lot in defining both the means and the relations of production but the latter were also determined by many other factors, particularly the nature of property relations and the distribution of land and other productive assets, the role of the State in this respect, and the conditions shaping monopoly formations in different societies. Furthermore, there did exist the socialist alternative and, though in a much less clear-cut manner, certain Third World alternatives. Now and in the coming years these legal and political (as well as social) diversities within the capitalist model and beyond it are likely to be influenced and driven forward by technology fixes dictated by the advance guard of capitalist development. The model of capitalism that seeks to penetrate and integrate the whole world is fundamentally a technological model.

Institutional Domain

Second, there has taken place a major transformation in the institutional domain within which world capitalism has been advancing. The emergence of multinational corporations as dominant structures within which technological development, scientific Research and Development

(R&D) as well as capital accumulation and fiscal modelling of the economy are taking place has changed many of the 'rules of the game' under capitalism. The MNC represents a major mutation in the evolution of human institutions and macro social and economic structures, and it influences the nature of the State in diverse settings.

Third, and this follows from the first two dimensions, capitalism is both itself becoming integrationist and rendering other structures of trade and commerce integrationist as well, either undermining or co-opting hitherto unintegrated economic and social structures. That such an integrative thrust will leave out large sections of different societies and particularly the poor as well as peripheral communities (tribal, forest-based, nomadic and others) is of course true. But when one talks of the world capitalist system one is not talking of the world as a whole but only that part of it which has access to the modern State, the modern Market and modern technology. Those who cannot join this powerful drive towards restructuring human arrangements will have to fend for themselves as in any case they are not only marginal but for most purposes redundant and unwanted.

Homogenization

Fourth, central to the drive towards integrating diverse societies into a world market is the single most powerful engine of homogenizing the globe: consumerism and its enormous spread across societies and across classes. By making everyone, irrespective of social background or demographic characteristics, want the same things and catch up with those who have already had them, consumerism has become the dominant engine of the growth of modern capitalism.

Fifth, such a model of capitalism depends very much on the revolution in communications and information technology that is also penetrating diverse societies and reducing them all to a few common denominators.

Penetrating the Peripheries

And finally, as part of the new economic and political imperium known as 'globalization', there is taking place a growing colonization of rural hinterlands and land masses. For a long time these had been left out of the global capitalist thrust as they were thought too backward or unavailable to industrial and commercial penetration. But with the growing importance of the consumer tastes of the new style world middle class in the overall scheme of things—with its mix of at once homogenized and ethnicized gratification of greed and avarice—there has taken place quite a change in the attitude towards the exploitation of rural farm lands, wastelands, social forestry areas and even deserts, as well as, of course, riverbeds and oceans, each of them becoming a 'resource' for ever new goodies and enticements. The global capitalist class is also becoming the global land-grabber (Pepsi is only the forerunner of a lot more to come) and the global merchant in the produce and loot of natural resources and the environment of the Third World. No wonder then that slogans like land reforms are making no headway anywhere any more. Also, no wonder that more and more proposals for investments and collaborations from abroad are directed to the consumer needs of the consumer classes—and the yuppie-ized and touristy among them—and less and less towards the infrastructure and other projects of industrialization. The latter at least (despite unequal access to them and their greater accent on growth than on justice) could produce the economic conditions necessary for jobs and welfare in the long run. The former, on the other hand, make the poor and the artisan at once an object of intensified exploitation and growing dispensability.

Historical Overview

It is time we realized the larger import of these various dimensions of the integrative thrust of 'globalization'. We face an unprecedented consolidation of the imperial era, of world capitalism and of techno-hegemony, i.e., the displacement of political management and control by a technocratic élite which represents an entirely new phenomenon. It encompasses various major shifts in the organization of human affairs, not just the displacement of the State by the Market, but also of politics by techno-rationality, of plurality of cultures by a mono-culture, of horizontal 'structures' by a vertical 'pyramid' (put differently, of multipolarity by unipolarity), of the *greening* of the world which stresses diversity and spontaneity by its *whitening* which stresses integration and straitjacketing. The 'end of history' thesis is not to be laughed out; it represents and announces the end of the era not just of the socialist challenge to the capitalist world but also of multipolarity of the world, of the system of nation states. It has called into question a plurality of the world and the dispersal of power that had taken place following the Second World War. It is the return of the capitalist-colonial framework that Francis Fukuyama and other excited champions of Western capitalism are celebrating.

Here it may be worthwhile to take cognizance of recent history in world affairs, of the growth and consolidation of the world system, and the present crisis in it, and of the most recent effort to deal with the crisis both ideologically and in terms of public policy (national and international). We need to explore the earlier correlation of forces after the Second World War that allowed an expansion of the West (of a more benign type) as compared to today's expansion of a more coercive and aggrandizing type. There were a number of reasons that made this possible. First, there was the tremendous success of post-Keynesian capitalism—on the one hand generating enough surplus and producing an unprecedented 'boom' in the capitalist countries, and on the other hand, willing (even if accepted reluctantly by some sections) to build a 'Welfare State', develop a framework of industrial relations and, in the bargain ensure a long era of industrial peace, making the working class itself accept the bourgeois democratic model of the State. This led to a large expansion of internal markets in these countries based on the purchasing power of the working class, yet providing sufficient scope for increased profits and capital accumulation, in turn also expanding externally through a new package of neo-colonialism in which the working class (and the peasantry) in the North became willing partners in the exploitation of the South.

It was a period of considerable consolidation and expansion of Western capitalism while at the same time giving it a 'human face' through the development of a globalist humanitarian ideology in the form of helping the poor of the world. There developed a series of institutional and policy initiatives—from the Truman Doctrine to Eisenhower's warning to the world of the growth of a military-industrial complex that had emerged in the West (as well as the East) to the highly attractive and enticing symbols generated during the Kennedy era. It was also a period that enabled the capitalist system to respond to and at the same time contain voices of dissent at home—from civil rights to the anti-Vietnam movement to environmentalism, feminism and anti-militarism.

Second, the advocacy of liberal democracy coupled with a 'mixed economy' opened up new vistas for capitalism in parts of the Third World (India being a prime example of this) in which the State itself provided major incentives and resources for capitalist expansion. Over time, as we can now see, through the growing appeal of the paradigm of technology, such an expansion paved the way for both government and industry in the Third World to become part of the global framework of capitalism.

The fact is that the newly independent states of the Third World which had at one time claimed that they would follow an independent path of development (some of them called it 'the third way', still others talked of 'delinking' from the North) failed to generate a real alternative. And, they ultimately accepted the dominant model of capitalist development propagated by the academic think-tanks of the West which facilitated the integrationist thrust of corporate capitalism. There is of late a partnership developing between the Third World bureaucratic colonial State and transnational capital and technology, with a few highly advertised cases of 'success', especially in South-East and East Asia but also in parts of Latin America. This has made others (who had opted to be both less brutal *vis-à-vis* their own people and less willing to allow multinational penetration) look like failures and, lacking confidence in their own vision and perspective and the capacity to hold on to their own distinctive models, ultimately made them too want to 'catch up' and hence get co-opted.

That in this whole change in perspective the 'social question' was shelved or rather that the technological model overtook the social model was not sufficiently noted, even by dissident and opposition forces, and even less by the international alternatives movement, is only part of the co-optation model. The latter had in the meanwhile got sidelined by preoccupation with other issues—environment, the status of women, disarmament and the like. Unfortunately, Marxism also failed to respond adequately to this knuckling under by so many countries that were once committed to finding alternatives to the capitalist model. And, before you knew it, came the collapse of the very citadels of socialism.

Underlying such an economic transformation has been a major shift in ideological thinking, starting in the West, then expanding globally. First in parts of the Third World where the appeal of liberalization had started growing since the mid-1970s. And then to the socialist world starting with some countries in Eastern Europe where Stalinist excesses had left deep scars and the demonstration effect of Western consumerism had made bigger inroads than in either the former Soviet Union or China, in Cuba or Nicaragua. And then again, with the collapse of the Soviet Union itself, both strategically and ideologically, throughout the rest of the Third World, not excluding China and India, the two countries that had stood for so long for (though very differently from each other) alternative models of 'indigenous' development.

Right Reaction

The 'Right Reaction' first emerged in the West. It was a reaction against the Welfare State and the modern ideas of distributive justice. It was also a reaction against the growing power of the poor, the minorities (especially the blacks in the US), the Third World lobby, the United Nations—especially the United Nations Conference on Science and Technology for Development (UNCTAD), the United Nations Educational, Scientific, and Cultural Organization (Unesco), the International Labour Organization (ILO), the United Nations International Children's Emergency Fund (Unicef) and the like which were seen to be partial to the Third World—and generally against the so-called radical intellectuals. It was an effort to bolster the somewhat weakening military-industrial complex by co-opting a whole lot of strategic thinkers, eminent economists and technocrats (many of them from India) and other professionals as consultants and members of advisory bodies. We have an emerging global professional élite which is indeed truly 'global' and which along with other groups (government bureaucrats and media representatives) serves the cause of transnational capitalism.

Whereas the power and reach of corporate capitalism has been on the ascendancy over time, despite challenges to it from both political and intellectual circles, what made it a vehicle of Right Reaction is the powerful and highly aggressive ideological twist given to it by Reaganism and Thatcherism on the one hand and the new phase of Bretton Woods institutions on the other. (There is reason to believe that President Reagan talked the World Bank officialdom out of supporting Third World states and leaning towards an ideology of 'privatization'.) Those who talk of the reduced economic power of the US do not reckon with the powerful *institutional* power that the US alone—the US State—wields. This covers a wide variety of fields. Obviously, the most important is the military-strategic one. However, it also obtains in the case of the international credit institutions in which financial resources of Europe and Japan are also mobilized but the main control continues to be with the Americans. This is the case with global economic diplomacy and the international trade regime (despite the war of nerves going on at GATT), the international banking regime which is very much controlled from the United States (both major commercial banks and of course the World Bank), and international lending and debt regimes, mainly through the IMF and various aid-consortia, as well. American hegemony is at once strategic, financial and commercial and its basic clout is institutional. It is a hegemony that has so far been unaffected by the recession in the West and the US itself, the growing fiscal imbalances and all the social costs that American citizens are paying (rising unemployment, race riots, homelessness and the erosion of poverty programmes).

The liberalization-privatization-globalization construct that is being offered to major countries of the Third World and the socialist world (including China and Russia) is part of this spreading Right Reaction. In fact, paradoxically, while it started in the hegemonic citadels of global power, it is making particular inroads in the two erstwhile alternative blocs that at one time held the promise of countering world hegemony by the West, namely the East on the one hand and the South on the other. It appears as if these former bastions of alternative paradigms are more available for the new ideologies of Right Reaction than the dominant centres themselves. The defeat suffered by the British Prime Minister, John Major, on the miners' issue, the recent gentle admonition by Chancellor Kohl to his partymen to be prepared to make sacrifices in living standards with a view to accommodating the interests of East Germans and other immigrants, or the whole debate in the US itself on the economic crisis arising from the deep debt in which Ronald Reagan and George Bush have left the country and the growing demand for the need for intervention by the federal government, are all indications of the end of the Reaganite hold. Also, as the economic crisis in the West deepens and affects more and more people, forcing them to reflect on the paradigm of liberalization and recall their own experience of the Great Depression and the fact that the way out of it was built on the ideas of Keynes and not of Hayek, they are beginning to reconsider things.

Unfortunately, such rethinking has not percolated to the ruling élite of Third World countries. Indeed, the real frontiers of the new economic ideology are to be found more in the South than in the North. It is here that the erosion of both our thinking as independent, post-colonial states and the alternative perspectives on development that we in our own confused way were experimenting with is taking place.

Counter-tendencies

Such a texturing of Third World prospects need not be accepted as something determined and irreversible. There is considerable flux in the current historical process, one that is inherently unstable and likely to give rise to growing class and ethnic conflicts. Already, the bullying methods employed by the US and US dominated agencies are producing countervailing forces and strengthening the voices of dissent that were there from the very beginning but were not heeded by national élites and bureaucrats and all but a few of the economists and social scientists. These dissenting voices are no longer that marginal or considered too 'idealistic' or motivated by dated ideological fixes.

Even the 'pragmatists' among policy-makers, public figures, writers and commentators in the mass media and other opinion makers are expressing doubts about the new package and getting alarmed at the price to be paid in respect of the autonomy and stability of the State that they were earlier willing to sacrifice at the altar of the Market. Meanwhile, the very regions that looked like having 'collapsed' before the march of the MNCs—Russia, Eastern Europe, China on the one hand and leading nations of the developing world on the other—are likely to face domestic pressures and unforeseen consequences of the new policies as well as nationalist protest against *Pax Americana.* This too will reinforce the forces of dissent and lend new legitimacy to those who had all along argued for an alternative model of development.

The basic assumption of the new policy package—more and more investment of capital from abroad and a wide welcome to India as an integral part of the global market—is already being questioned while in the meanwhile it has dealt serious damage to what had been a well thought out set of institutions and practices following the broad acceptance of the State as a pivot around which they had been structured. It was also a pivot around which international economic relations had evolved. The precipitate dismantling of so many bulwarks of accountability at home and immunity from external influences is going to make us highly vulnerable to the latter and increasingly fragile and destabilized internally. With all this, restlessness and public protest will be on the increase and there will take place a climactic crash of the so-called 'radical alternative' of structural adjustment and globalization.

The same State or rather the government is also being subjected to other pressures—GATT, Super 301 the rocket deal (with Russia), Nuclear Non Proliferation Treaty (NPT), falling in line in voting at the United Nations, making us move away from the non-aligned movement and G 77 and soliciting our mediation with radical regimes in the Third World on behalf of the world status quo. Such a turn around in positions and postures is going to be too much to take, even by the corrupt consumer middle class that had provided solid support to the new policies to begin with. And as far as the poorer classes and the unemployed youth are concerned, the response is likely to be more than that of mere discontent and disenchantment. While on the social plane it will be increasingly class based and violent, on the regional plane it will strengthen demands for autonomy and self-determination and will seek support from human rights movements among minority, tribal and nationality groupings. But, of course, both of these can also play into the hands of fundamentalist and chauvinist tendencies.

Meanwhile, as the 'new' hegemonic world order becomes more and more unstable, it will make political and professional élites in countries like ours feel even more insecure and entrapped in the global financial and commercial structure of dependency. Squeezed between internal revolt and external commitments, the institutions of the State will become more and more fragile and unable to hold things together. Only then will the futility of the old order (of which the so-called 'new policy package' is an integral part) dawn on those who had somehow, despite all indications to the contrary, kept believing in the virtues of world capitalism.

Prospects for Alternative Formations—How Feasible?

Whether the mainstream democratic process will be able to provide relevant alternatives within the established institutional order by throwing up new political formations and class alignments remains to be seen. There is quite a large constituency available both at the grassroots and at the macro and intermediate levels for this to take off but it is still a highly fragmented terrain. It (i.e., the alternatives movement) faces the further task of either once again partially delinking from the global market and other structures of world governance (on which, despite early gains, it has not been able to carry the governments and professional élites of the South) or transforming the latter on the basis of a new ideological and institutional framework. Unfortunately, despite a whole spate of theorizing over twenty years for an alternative vision and an alternative set of institutions, even the beginnings of a new ideological consensus in this regard have yet to take place. The global institutions of finance capital, its technological underpinning and political support structure *do* have an ideological consensus, and a strong confidence in being able to spread it across the world. That it cannot provide an enduring basis for peace and justice and hence cannot survive for long is, of course, clear. But when it all begins to shake and even seems like moving towards a crash, will we be ready with a well thought out alternative, a political and communications strategy to make it sound both right and workable, and a policy framework for translating it into agendas of action?

The alternative to being prepared with such an alternative will only be widespread chaos, uncontrollable violence and growing trade and commerce in such violence. Needless to say, the worst sufferers of such a collapse of civil society will be the poor, and among the poor, women and children and the aged and the handicapped. Working toward an intellectual framework for an alternative is by no means a luxury. It is needed above all by the victims of history.

The Political System and the Poor

Before we turn to the issues and considerations that it is necessary to deal with in order to move towards such an intellectual framework, we must analyse the growing assault on basic institutions—for long organized around the modern State—as an inherent feature of the new perspective on organizing the human enterprise, namely the political implications thereof from the point of view of the poor and oppressed sections of countries of the Third World like India. Turning our back on the basic challenge of social transformation through the institutions of the State that we had both conceived and sought to build when we became independent, has led to another major consequence for a polity that calls itself a democracy. Both the growing divide between integrated classes and disinherited masses and the serious erosion of the environment, social diversity and cultural roots of diverse populations will, of necessity, lead to a gradual erosion of and a mounting attack on human rights and the democratic framework within which people could find a meaningful existence in an environment of freedom and dignity.

The limits of a formal electoral and representative democracy which fails to fulfil people's aspirations for the betterment of their living conditions and to provide a sense of justice and fair play are already becoming clear. An electoral democracy uninformed by a commitment to justice and a decentralized political order in which the people are themselves allowed to make decisions that affect them is bound to produce manipulative politics, and the phenomenon of criminalization of not just the polity but of society as a whole, including of the poor and unemployed (or the heavily underemployed) strata who themselves get inducted into the politicization of the criminal and violent type. Their search for livelihood is monetized through the sheer need for cash through which they can then buy not just food and the other essentials of livelihood but also the new goodies offered by the modern market. Consumerism and criminalization have thus become two facets of a social order that has lost its moorings and is instead led towards integration into an alien marketplace. It is in this manner that commodity fetishism takes over people and communities that had for long sustained themselves in austere and modest but dignified lifestyles that were close to nature and grounded in culture and its diverse spiritual sensibilities. The loss of human rights and access to democratic spaces, following the penetration of external and alien markets into relatively self-reliant village communities, leads to such a loss of value and sensibilities. Behind it all lies the decline and undermining of the larger political process and the institutions that had enabled that process to reach out to more and more people, including and more particularly to the poor and exploited sections of society. No amount of plans and schemes for 'alleviating' poverty can succeed without empowering the people with basic political rights and providing them with a stake in the political order. This has by now become quite clear.

The political dimensions of poverty have hardly ever been brought out in their fullness either by economists working on poverty (on which they are supposed to be experts) or by those (mainly bureaucrats) who have been entrusted with the task of implementing various programmes aimed at reducing 'levels' of poverty or promoting employment and ensuring minimum incomes or equipping the deprived with the necessary skills and capacities. How much one wishes that these bearers of the burden of alleviating poverty by the State told us why they have failed so miserably! Lacking such insights, there has taken place a growing disability of the political system alongside the growing destabilization of civil society at all levels (from family to community to region to the 'nation' as a whole). This disability will only get accentuated as a consequence of sharply rising unemployment and an increasingly disenchanted, insecure and angry youth, a rapid breakdown in living conditions, a growing decay of the physical environment, and an increasing incidence of squalor and disease and insufferable surroundings in both rural habitats and urban ghettos to which this youth is forced to migrate, following the almost total erosion of the environment and the weakening of community ties.

Inevitably, all this is producing explosive situations and a generalized state of lumpenization which is taking hold of both mainstream politics and the politics of revolt and rebellion as well as producing highly communal and chauvinistic movements. In short, as said earlier, the result is the lumpenization and criminalization of not just politics but the social fabric itself. Intertwined as such a decline in civility is with the growing neglect by the State of the poor and victimized sections and given the increasing identification in the public mind of the 'State' with the police and para-military forces as well as the army (all of them not just permitting and overlooking but often themselves indulging in rape and loot and murder), it is not surprising that the youth in particular is under pressure to increasingly gravitate towards militancy. The latter is taking both a regional ('terrorist') and a social (Naxalite) form or, alternately, and unfortunately more frequently, highly communal and chauvinistic modes of 'revolt' against the system.

The World We tried to Build

Such far-reaching implications for States, cultures and peoples of the privatization and globalization model and of the growing amnesia about poverty and injustice are also reflected in a rapid and dramatic restructuring of the global institutional order itself. The international system that had emerged after the Second World War was by no means just and equitable but nonetheless had certain in-built balances. There was even a tripolar world order which was characterized by both the East-West and the North-South balances as well as by a global and a regional institutional structure represented by the United Nations and allied agencies. Both the 'bipolarity' and the 'multipolarity' of the world institutional structure had provided nations of the Third World with opportunities for exercising leverages which, in the course of time, led to periodic assertions by major nations of the Third World in the flow of contemporary history. The United Nations and other similar structures—UNCTAD, ILO, Unesco, Unicef, United Nations Environment Programme (UNEP), Food and Agriculture Organization (FAO), even UNDP—provided a lot of space to representatives of the Third World and non governmental organizations (NGOs) and committed intellectuals from all parts of the world to inject ideas and perspectives that were designed to create a more just and humane world. They were also able to join intellectuals and activists from the North who were interested in limiting the dangers inherent in a world dominated by the two super powers and their strategists who were steadily transferring resources that should have gone towards increasing human welfare to endless acquisition of armaments from which the Third World itself was not immune.

The ideological thinking that had emerged from the growth of the Welfare State in the West and the national liberation movements in the South as well as the 'socialist alternative' that was being attempted in the East were all playing their roles in modifying the aggressive postures and enmities of mere 'bipolarity'. This also gave rise to a series of initiatives and assertions, mostly from the South but also, in response thereto, from the North. The non-aligned movement, the G-77, the regional consolidations of Third World states and the considerable use of debates in UNCTAD, the ILO, Unicef and Unesco in which intellectuals and diplomats from the Third World played their role, all led to a culture of dialogue and negotiations which allowed the poor countries to place on the agenda of the world issues of equity, justice and cultural integrity. In the economic arena also, though the results were by no means satisfactory and often produced a lot of distortions, there was continuous pressure on the affluent parts of the world. There took place an effort to sensitize them to the plight of the poorer parts of the world to which of course their response was at once limited and mechanistic: a package of aid, liberalized trade, technology transfers and the creation of global funds in a variety of areas ranging from food to environment. Yet, while much of this exhibited a combination of ulterior and benign motives, it did create an environment of collective endeavour on the part of the élites of the world. In bringing it about the former Soviet Union and other socialist countries did not play a direct role. And yet the reality of a 'bipolar', in effect a tripolar, world contributed to efforts at reducing extremes of disparity and exploitative structures.

The World Now in the Making

As was mentioned earlier, today we have arrived at a threshold of history in which all of this is in a shambles and, what is worse, it is in a shambles not just because of the doings of the powerful but also because of those who are supposed to represent poorer nations and peoples. As the world that came into being after the Second World War and during the long period of the Cold War lies in a shambles—following the collapse of the Socialist 'bloc' as a counter-force to the Western hegemony bloc and the virtual collapse of the Third World as an alternative pivot of world opinion and world politics—new recipes for structuring it and providing it with a new doctrine of survival and 'progress' have emerged. This is the doctrine of globalized, liberalized regimes and privatized development, together producing an integrated 'world order', the chief engineers of which are to be the MNCs. It is of course true that while liberalization is propagated for the Third World to adopt, monopolistic devices and protectionist barriers will continue to be indulged in by the dominant countries. But this does not seem to worry the propagators of world capitalism and 'world order'. For them such devices are necessary to protect the capitalist countries both from fresh invasions from the Third World and from each other (US vs. Europe vs. Japan vs. the newly industrialized countries of Asia). As liberalization advances, we are told, and as Third World élites are able to integrate themselves into the world market and accept its discipline, and as the internal competition within the advanced capitalist world is sorted out, we will all be in a better position in a new and dynamic—and presumably constantly growing—world economy.

The full maturity of world capitalism, advanced technology and transnational corporations is something that is still in the process of being worked out. Its eventual fruition will depend a lot on the willing acceptance by the poorer parts of the world of the new model. If they resist or if they try to take advantage of divisions or differences within the advanced capitalist world, they will only prevent the smooth transition from a State-oriented and zero-sum world to a truly market based and non-zero-sum, and hence benign and peaceful, world. A whole generation has been lost in the futile game of competing ideologies and doctrinaire nationalisms. The time has come to move out of the conflicts and confrontations that this had involved and towards a new and beneficial world order. So we are told.

That the acceptance of the new model of growth and governance entails massive change and quite a degree of destablization of the established order (both domestic and international), including major turn arounds in priorities and perspectives is, no doubt, quite clear. But it is being persistently advocated by the votaries of 'structural adjustment' and 'structural reform', that have been conceived to restructure the global economic and political framework. And these votaries are to be found both globally and locally, the latter more often than not tutored by the former, but convinced of the rightness of the path that has been advocated, or so they are led to think.

The System under Stress

According to conventional wisdom, it is the élites who want stability while the masses are interested in change, and the more high the élites, the more the desire for stability. However, as we look at the reality as it is unfolding in countries of the Third World, it is becoming increasingly clear that there seems to be growing interest in destabilizing established institutional orders (global and national) on the part of élites, in undermining the rules of the game on which they were based, particularly in systems that were somewhat democratic and in which the State was entrusted with the task of intervening on behalf of the poor. On the contrary, it is the masses that are bound to suffer from the resulting instabilities and decline of institutions and the basic consensus on which they are based. Both the élites and the people at large—particularly the poor, the minorities, the women—feel insecure but it is the former who can arm themselves with 'security' while it is the latter who face the crisis of survival and lose both their freedom and autonomy and, in many cases, their lives (*their* security). They are also unable to carry on with their normal activities and persist in their efforts at improving their living conditions. At the same time they are faced by another source of insecurity which seems to be spreading rather fast, namely growing communalism and the rise of 'fundamentalist' appeals which are continuously disrupting their lives and living conditions, sometimes also, unfortunately, drawing them into a vortex of sectarian politics and religious fanaticism. It is the poor who unknowingly become the victims of all vicious trends—secular (i.e., economic and market-propelled) and sectarian.

All in all, then, there seems to have set in a gradual (sometimes imperceptible, sometimes quite manifest) process of dissolution of the binding nexus of survival in a society which had, despite its injustices and inequities, provided a framework within which diverse communities found a place. It was expected that the promise of democracy and of an egalitarian social order would provide a better and more progressive basis for survival (survival in the dynamic sense of the term), in particular through the institutionality of a positive State. Instead, in the bargain, they (the diverse communities) seem to have lost both their freedom to manoeuvre in their respective arenas and their security in the arena supposed to be provided by the State. On the contrary, the arena of the State is getting increasingly authoritarian and repressive, the central authority in particular being once more on the rampage against vulnerable people and communities, now in close concert with the market and monopoly forces pressing hard on it. It is also found to be engaged in an attack on human rights organizations which are engaged in protecting the rights of the deprived and of increasingly marginalized sections of society, an attack in which the mass media (a large majority of them) seem to be joining.

Those who are engaged in such a systematic onslaught on the poor and deprived sections of society do not seem to realize the costs of what they are doing. As the sense of insecurity among the people grows, alongside persisting poverty, unemployment and increasing injustice and discrimination, it pushes the poor and the unemployed into a culture of protest, anger and desperation, contributing further to an overall condition of insecurity which is then exploited by sectarian politicians and is sought to be put down by a criminalized police and para-military establishment. Slowly and without their knowing it, the poor are being pushed into a world of crime and criminality, of inter-ethnic violence and militancy against the State.

It is this wanton criminalization of poverty spurred on by the politics of the élite that poses the most fundamental crisis of survival. It also poses a serious crisis in the system and its stability. If the poor have no recognized institutional channels through which to take up their grievances against the continuous injustices that they face, and if the élite no longer consider it necessary to act through the same institutions and their systems of accountability—they already seem to be acting more and more outside the institutional framework thereby reducing their legitimacy—there seems to be less and less scope for improving the condition of the people through the operation of the existing order. Hence the growing appeal of radical movements all round the country, including those that are engaged in insurgency against the State and even those that are engaged in mindless violence in which ordinary people also get hurt. There is no reason for the poor and for others (minorities, the tribals, women) to join anti-systemic forces for they have everything to lose by joining them. For them, in fact, the best course is to work through the system and try and bend it towards policies and programmes designed to improve both the living conditions and political clout of the large majority of the people. It is also a fact that at least till now the suffering sections of the Indian population have pinned their hopes on the State, the political system created by it, and whatever remains of its institutions, be it the Parliament, the courts or the electoral system itself. (The continuing large turnouts at the time of elections, except of course the illegitimate ones like those that were held in Tripura, Kashmir and Punjab at different times, is largely because of the continuing faith of the poor in the system.)

Refocusing the System?

To me it seems that the Constitution and the democratic institutions left to us by the first generation of nation-builders, with all their shortcomings, still provide a broad framework within which policies and actions that can improve the condition of the poor and make them full citizens of this land of ours (at present they are treated as marginal and even dispensable) can be devised and vigorously pursued. But for this to happen the system will have to move towards clear and definite interventions by the State on behalf of those who have over the last couple of decades been more or less excluded from both the process of development and access to political and administrative structures. The only way of preventing the poor, the minorities, the tribals and other deprived strata from being so excluded and then forced to turn against the system, is to restore the institutional framework of democracy and the political mandate laid out in the Indian Constitution. The urgent need facing the country, far more than servicing our external debts, is to redeem our pledges to the people and make them feel, once again, part of a larger social and political order. It also follows that for this to happen we cannot any longer rely on indirect and so-called 'long term' policies for the eradication of poverty and the rise in employment and other opportunities. What we need is a direct and immediate focus on the removal of poverty and the reduction of disparities, and on dealing with the socio-cultural expressions of human misery caused despite (some would say because of) decades of planning and the pursuit of growth and prosperity.

Such a direct and immediate focus will have to be essentially political in nature. While no doubt strategies of accumulation, dispersal and distribution of wealth based on appropriate economic models and choices of technologies will be needed, the basic goals and policy priorities will have to be set and basic decisions both made and implemented by the intellectual and political leadership as is already evident from the oft-repeated emphasis on 'political will' by planners and economists.

Historical Experience

A quick glance at the historical experience of Europe will bear this out. In Europe, the phenomenon of poverty has been dealt with in three stages. At first it was through charity and welfare measures adopted by a paternalistic upper class, often through the agency of the State. This was during the eighteenth and early nineteenth centuries during which, for instance, 'poor houses' were set up in England and other similar institutions elsewhere in Europe. The starving and miserable poor were provided with food and other necessities in these houses. There was as yet no general abundance of resources nor any clear ideology on distributing the social product. On the other hand, there had already begun a mass exodus from the countryside to the cities following the Enclosures Movement and the growth in population.

There followed the Industrial Revolution and the concomitant process of accumulation of capital and large increases in 'surplus value' which made the European societies (in stages, starting with Great Britain) prosperous and affluent. This was also helped by a series of bourgeois revolutions, the most important of which was the French Revolution, which removed feudal impediments and culture in which slavery and bondage were preferred to individual freedom and well-being, preferred also to the generation of agricultural surpluses for the landowning class itself (as with our own *zamindars* who are keener on holding on to bonded labour than on raising productivity). While this may have released productive forces for the bourgeoisie, there was as yet no well-defined strategy for the distribution of wealth and resources from the rich who had benefited from the new prosperity to the poor. In fact, as a series of studies starting from the monumental work of Karl Marx have shown, the Industrial Revolution was accompanied by, and to some extent fueled by, the exploitation of the working classes.

In course of time, alongside the growth of mass poverty in an era of economic expansion and prosperity, there also took place the phenomenon of 'business cycles', of periods of economic expansion and boom followed by those of depression and 'crash' of the stock market, the latter to some extent because of the exploitative character of a system which did not permit sufficiently large markets (based on the expansion of purchasing power among the labouring classes) to grow and gave rise to monopolistic tendencies. With both the growth of poverty and mass misery, overcrowding and the growth of slums in the cities, high rates of unemployment during periods of depression and the resulting civil strife and industrial unrest, there emerged the need for the State to step in to release productive forces from monopolistic control and reduce the vast gaps that divided the social classes. There was as yet no doctrine of 'socialism' as was to happen later. If anything, the State was called upon to assist in the growth of capitalist development both by overcoming its periodic 'crises' and being called upon to assist in the growth of ancillary services like banking, insurance, security against the large liquidation of business concerns and other institutional devices to contain the risks inherent in capitalist growth, as well as—later on—in the laying out of basic infrastructures for industries and their maintenance and investment in long-gestation projects that private investors were not willing to build.

The State in Europe was in fact to serve the capitalist cause much more than this. It was to facilitate the colonization of distant lands and forests, the growth of a plantation economy, access to the raw materials and markets of the colonized lands and, through all this, to enable home countries to spread the benefits of capitalism to the lower classes and thus contain the class struggles that were inherent in the capitalist model. This ensured the rise of all round affluence in Western Europe and the United

States, and later in Japan though the growth of capitalism in the latter took a somewhat different turn from that of the West.

The affluent nations faced perhaps the most serious economic crisis in their history in 1929 and continuing through the Thirties—during the same period as the rise of Fascism and Nazism on the one hand and consumerism on the other. The answer to this crisis did not emerge from within the framework of economic development but largely from outside it. This, with the political intervention of the State, much larger than ever before, in the process transforming the capitalist structure and imparting new dynamics to the capitalist system, and so saving it from collapse. This was the result of the almost revolutionary role played by Keynesianism, giving rise to the 'New Deal' of President Roosevelt in the United States and the modern Welfare State in Western Europe. Those Western thinkers who are today advocating a return to free trade and the free market as a way out of the economic crises facing Third World countries and asking for a drastic reduction in the role of the State need to be reminded of their own history and experience in dealing with economic crises which also happened to be at bottom financial crises and crises of growing indebtedness.

New Developments

With the above account of economic development and the role of the State in Europe, however, the story of European and American capitalism is by no means complete. By the time the recovery from the Great Depression had taken place, and was followed by the impact of the Second World War on the locus of political and economic power in the West (in the main, shifting the locus from Europe to the United States and, in military terms, to the US and the Soviet Union), two new developments appeared on the horizon. The first of these was the emergence on the world scene of independent but on the whole poor countries. The second was the growing ideological warfare between the two super powers, leading to the militarization of large parts of the world. There was also, of course, the problem of reviving the war-shattered economies but while the Marshall Plan, based on the pumping of dollars into West European economies, energized Europe and galvanized its latent capital and technological resources into an era of quick abundance, the presumably corresponding plan for the much poorer parts of the world, namely the Truman Doctrine, failed miserably in fulfilling its proclaimed objectives based as they were on the pumping of foreign aid into the countries of the Third World. This was both because of the diversion of massive resources to the pursuit of the Cold War (including military expenditure in the Third World) and the creation, because of this, of two opposite consequences for two sets of countries.

The first set consisted of the countries of the South that benefited from the Korean, Vietnamese and many other wars and war-like situations, and the various regional military pacts, as also from large-scale economic transfers and investments from the United States and other Western countries. These countries were South Korea, Taiwan, Hong Kong, Singapore, Malaysia and, to a lesser extent, Thailand, Indonesia and the Philippines. The same happened earlier on a much larger scale with Japan. (That most of these countries, with the exception of Japan, have paid serious political costs arising from lop-sided capitalist development and the rise of authoritarian regimes which, according to some Western thinkers, are necessary to push high rates of growth will be examined a little later.) The second set consisted of countries that did not receive such massive infusions and were also not willing to become vassals of American imperial power, but at the same time fell for the development model that was sold to them by Western scholars, foreign foundations and foundation-sponsored experts and continued to drift in a dualist stream of 'development'. All the efforts put in by the United Nations and donor agencies proved of no avail. On the contrary, they reinforced the dualism and pushed these countries towards a perverse form of Keynesianism which only increased the power of the business and corporate class and made the State itself increasingly bureaucratized and corrupt and, in the course of time, served the interests of the same corporate class.

The strategies of self-reliance and 'collective self-reliance' that were proposed by some Third World thinkers failed to give rise to a redistributive State and instead gave rise to the loss of legitimacy of a State which had become highly centralized and corrupt and a similar loss of legitimacy of a socialist alternative to capitalism given the failure of the latter to provide minimum freedoms to their peoples as well as the failure to fulfil growing economic aspirations. Both these sets of failure—in effect, the failure of the State in both the socialist and the Third World countries—paved the way for the revival and rapid spread of the old and already failed doctrine of free trade and the Market, with the added dimension of 'globalization' to the earlier theories of liberalization and privatization. The new economic policies based on the Market are to be carried out not by diverse governments of nation states or even local capitalist enterpreneurs but by the newly discovered engine of growth round the world, namely the multinational corporations with which local business and bureaucracies are being asked to fall in line.

I have argued elsewhere that the decline in the legitimacy of the State was first a result of the critique from the left and liberal intellectuals and parties which were opposed to the over-centralization and élitism of the State which had ceased to serve the interests of the poor but it (i.e., decline in the legitimacy of the State) was used more effectively by the right. Hence the benefit of the same has gone to the proponents of the Market and particularly the MNCs rather than to the institutions of civil society and to a decentralized social and political order. With this new direction of the argument for an alternative to existing policies, whatever little social purpose there was to the earlier model of development and the role of the State in it is sought to be given up. And with that, of course, the whole concern with poverty and inequity is played down.

Based on the above analysis of the pursuit of prosperity and of poverty arising out of the same, both within and across societies and states, I can now return to the earlier theme of the politics of poverty, including the politics of countering it. We have seen that poverty as a state of affairs—as a description of social stratification—may be an economic reality at a particular point of time. But both its origin and its perpetuation—or accentuation—must be located in the nature of the political process. In short, poverty over a long period of time or as a continuing characteristic of a given society is at bottom the political condition in which it finds itself. It is a condition that arises out of a given structure of power and opportunities and its mitigation depends on capacities to intervene by political actors. These actors could be the institutions of the State and the élite in control of these institutions, deciding to enforce a constitutional mandate or a mandate given by the people to a governing or an oppositional élite. Failing this, the acts of intervention pass on to sections of the people most likely drawn from the poor and the hitherto powerless themselves, though in historically rare situations where a high degree of sensitivity or commitment exists among other social strata, to the middle and professional classes and those whose youth was influenced by idealistic currents of thought. These strata may also intervene on behalf of the poor and for the creation of a just and egalitarian society. Realistically, perhaps, we need a combination of both types of interventionary acts.

The reason for the necessity of people themselves intervening in the political process arises out of the fact that although the removal of poverty can to a large extent be a function of the pursuit of 'distributive justice' and of the removal of concentrations of wealth and means of production in a few hands, it entails much more than the mere distribution of largesse by the government and other institutions of the State. We have already indicated that while the role of the State in intervening in the development process on behalf of the poor and the underprivileged sections of society must continuously be insisted upon, there are serious limits to what the State can achieve in the absence of a revolutionary transformation of civil society. We have also seen that the State has increasingly become highly centralized and its institutions have moved further and further away from the people so that it is no longer a liberating force which is able to take society out of its unjust and iniquitous character. This, despite some symbolic gestures like programmes designed to help specific social groups as, for instance, special reservations for the Dalits and the tribals. We have also seen that the ills of a centralized and increasingly corrupt state apparatus cannot be undone by going for the model of integration into a world market that is free from interventions by national governments as the latter is only likely to centralize power and opportunities still further and restrict the scope of participation by the people in the development process or in governance and decision-making.

The Indian Experience

These observations have a particular bearing for a country like India for which both a centralized State and a globalist Market are alien phenomena. What held this civilization together and enabled it to survive longer than any other was a unique culture which was at once pluralistic and decentralized, in which there was no one centre that dominated all others. It was because of this that it was able to absorb a variety of new social and cultural streams from abroad. It was also because of this that it was able to integrate such a variety of social and economic strata including the less fortunate ones, despite the inherent inequality of a hierarchical social order. Belonging to specific communities that existed with a pluralistic and decentralized order reduced the sense of injustice and enabled individuals and groups belonging to the 'lower' social strata to make demands on the larger society. There being no clear centre, there were also no pronounced peripheries. Similarly, there being no central thrust towards things like progress and prosperity, there was no strong feeling of being left out of the same. To the extent that there was such a feeling, it was of a different type and was expressed in a different way, generally through efforts at social mobility and over a period of time by changing the nature of the hierarchical order in the same system.

It was the British who for the first time brought together the various communities and kingdoms under a single 'Raj'. Many parts of this were governed indirectly but there is no doubt that a major consolidation was carried out in the form of a unified entity called India. But even this was not yet a nation state that evoked feelings of belonging or being left out. What was left behind by the British was not a polity but an administration along with the police and the army. The British also left behind a system, of justice and civil authority although the latter was largely provincial and local (district and below). It was the transfer of power to a political élite that had emerged out of a long struggle for independence that brought legitimacy to the Centre. It was this political élite that both during and after independence laid out the broad ideology of democratic nation-building which, apart from involving the people in the political process, also undertook the task of removing poverty and raising the standards of living of the people.

Poverty removal was thus conceived as a political task and as a necessary component of democratic nation-building. However, almost from the beginning there was a serious flaw in the way this task was sought to be pursued. For the most part it was entrusted to a colonial administration and not a party or similar political instrument operating at different levels and interacting with diverse communities and peoples. It was this State-centred and bureaucratic model of development that simply failed to make any dent on poverty or other forms of injustice and discrimination despite all kinds of plans and programmes and schemes that have been launched time and again and despite a large array of legislative measures that have been put on the statute book. It was all too fragmentary an approach, lacking a core, vulnerable to all kinds of interests. The State became centralized without there being a central thrust that could unite the whole country into a single effort. Centralization without such a central thrust in which the people were participating also necessarily led to wide gaps developing between the Centre and the diverse regions and communities.

As for the administration, its not being directed politically at different levels continued its colonial form and even extended it further, and gradually made it less and less accountable and more corrupt. There were of course politicians all over the place but not being part of a defined political structure, they too were drawn into the same vortex of unaccountable and corrupt practices. Over time, the diverse regions and communities that had constituted the unique civilizational thrust on which a centralized administration was imposed tended to drift away and either challenged the authority of the Centre or simply moved out of its domain by not participating in its plans and programmes. Today the writ of the Centre does not run in many regions of the country. And this is largely the case because of a lack of understanding on the part of the élite of the basic nature of the society it was trying to administer.

The same analysis applies to the effort, currently under way, to impose an even more centralized (indeed globalized) Market. On the other hand, the effort to make poverty removal a populist, catch-all appeal, as was done with 'Garibi Hatao', only led to élitist rebounds: the failure of the 'Garibi Hatao' programme led, *reductio ad absurdum*, to the advocacy of liberalization and globalization. Again, what stood in the way of the 'Garibi Hatao' campaign (in which quite a few individuals and groups, and the people at large, had placed faith) was its failure to produce its own Keynesian programmes and corresponding institutional structures and legislative measures as was done under the New Deal in the US and in the evolution later of the Welfare State in large parts of Western Europe. This further reduced the legitimacy of State-sponsored initiatives and produced the euphoria about the liberalization doctrine and the so-called 'New Economic Package'.

We have then come through an experience which included the earlier model of development in which the State was to provide the 'commanding heights', the later political and egalitarian thrust which placed the initiative for poverty removal in the hands of a centralized and in fact highly personalized leadership, and now, with the collapse of both and the decline of faith in either of these, the attempt to go back to free trade and invite multinationals to bail us out—none of which inspires any hope. Indeed, all of them are together likely to lead us into a serious crisis of survival as a people and as a system, particularly from the point of view of facing up to the basic challenge of persisting poverty and disparities and of dealing with the growing sense of deprivation felt by growing numbers of people. The latter may well be forced into joining 'movements' that will only further destabilize the State and render it ineffective in handling the rising challenges to its authority which even the proponents of the Market would like the State to handle but which, because of the very consequences that will follow the policies advocated by them, such as growing unemployment and inflation, will hamstring the State.

It is important to grasp the cultural consequences of what has just been said, especially for a country like India endowed with unique historical and civilizational characteristics as were laid out earlier. A pluralist culture is not very well equipped to handle new types of disparities and social dissonance engendered by the globalist (as opposed to the earlier 'colonial') thrust. The ever deepening divides and schisms, especially of a material kind, tend to shatter the unity based on pluralities and diversities, produce large distortions in the very structure of society and generate a *political* process that is full of animosities, mutual distrust and ill-feeling (often verging on hatred) and confrontationist and extremist stances (religious fundamentalism being only one manifestation thereof), much of this becoming increasingly violent—a type of violence that cannot be brought under control by either the State or any erstwhile mechanisms of civil society. In fact, with its plural structure already under stress, the new types of disparities will only impair civil society. What is at work is a corrosive pincer: the homogenizing thrust of globalization on the one hand and the disintegrative thrust of social diversity on the other. It was the humane and egalitarian model of the State that could have—and for a long while did—held the two at bay. But it is precisely such a State that is now programmed to wither away, both its autonomy ('sovereignty') *vis-à-vis* the world at large and its autonomy *vis-à-vis* special interests at home (both traditional and modern).

In the debate over the new economic package and over the growing pressures on us as well as other Third World countries by the industrialized nations, there is a great deal of discussion on the issue of sovereignty. The reality is that we never really came out of the colonial grip. We have all along, both as a State and as an economy, been dependent on external models and resources. Furthermore, to the extent we had achieved a degree of autonomy and 'sovereignty', such as in our efforts to become self-reliant, we never thought of extending this autonomy and sovereignty and the self-reliance that we had achieved—or the security of the nation that was made possible by our application of national resources and science and technology to that end—to the people at large. So long as sovereignty, self-reliance and security are conceived in terms of the State alone, and that too a State that has increasingly alienated the mass of people and diverse communities and regions, it will not be possible to enthuse the people into thinking of them as something of value. The real issue is that we have been, both through the State and through the Market, both through centralization and through globalization, moving towards a condition of growing injustice, instability and insecurity, giving rise not to consensus but to confrontation, forcing the people to wage their diverse struggles for survival (both as individuals and as communities) without much hope of these being assisted by the élite strata of society, including the sizeable professional middle class, the mass media and the intelligentsia.

It is in this basic respect that issues like poverty need to be conceived fundamentally as political challenges which call for organized mobilization of the people against the special interests that have got entrenched in the system, both the old-style colonial administration and the new interests induced by external influences. For the fact is that these interests and this administration have already moved along a path that leaves out the poor and striving classes, a path that will only end in some form of social Darwinism and the 'survival of the fittest', pushing the rest into the dustbins of history.

The Emerging Class Ethos

The latest phase of such a strategy of 'survival of the fittest' presents itself in a rather attractive form, at least for the educated middle classes of the world, especially the professional and scientific segments thereof as well as for the managerial élite in diverse societies. The language in which it is presented is one of an 'integrative' and 'holistic' enterprise, presumably carrying everyone and every society forward in the process. The ruling classes have always, at various points in history, employed such jargon. Whether it be the 'Great Society' dream—and programme—of integrating the blacks and the urban poor into prosperous America or Rajiv Gandhi's dream of moving into the twenty-first century as a technologically advanced country that will be integrated into the world economy, the basic promise is for those who are already part of the mainstream. But it also appears to attract new entrants and aspirants—the upper and middle rungs of those who could escape from their diverse social settings, including the migrants who have left their rural habitats and, after a stint in urban slums, have made their way up into lower middle class colonies, or even the Dalits and the backwards who have, through reservations, education and urban mobility, moved into the same classes. It has also held an attraction for the various minorities.

For the rest, it is grinding poverty not just in economic per capita income terms but in the more basic sense of being discards of the social process—the outcastes, the dispensables, the victims of a social 'triage', and all this because of and not in spite of the modernizing drive on which the integrationist world-view is based.

The Middle Class Phenomenon

It is necessary to go into this phenomenon a little more closely. While for long a slow growing process of class formation, it is likely to prove highly unsettling and potentially explosive for society as a whole in the not too distant future. It arises from the growth of a middle class of the 'secularized' and English-educated (drawing with them the highly educated in other languages too), predominantly urban but at the same time having a stake in certain kinds of 'rural development'. There are tensions within this class too—communal, caste-based, professional as well as those arising from the very ethics of competition and upward mobility on which their rise had been based. But these are still tensions within the social structure of the successful, the affluent, the upwardly mobile and the *nouveau riche*. They are nothing as compared to the schism that divides this class from the poor who have remained or continue to be poor because they have been doomed by the very dynamics of 'development'. It is with the condition of the latter, their growing exclusion by the former and the increasing amnesia about their very existence by the ruling élite, officialdom and the mass media and hence by society at large that this book is concerned.

At one level what I am concerned with is a fundamentally moral issue: given this boiling conundrum in which we find ourselves, where do the leaders of society, especially those at the top who are entrusted with the agenda of social change—equity, justice, creating harmony and balance between warring communities, holding the nation together not by force but through the political process—stand? Where also do the leaders belonging to poor families and deprived social strata, having humble origins but now able to influence decisions and to some extent even policies, stand? And where do intellectuals, supposed to be the conscience-keepers of a society in flux, stand? All of them as passive bystanders and, directly or indirectly, beneficiaries and exploiters of the very divisions that are creating the growing chaos around them? Supporting one kind of populism or another, out of a feeling of sheer helplessness and despair and the increasing ruthlessness and amorality among all parties and most groups and 'movements', seeking a release from this increasingly unjust and oppressive nation state, through armed revolt if necessary, for separation or secession, for there is no hope under it? Or, at the other end of the spectrum, trying to get out of the mood of despair among the people, building on the feeling that 'things will work out after all', looking in the meanwhile for a leader with a capital 'L', or a party or an organization that promises to be tough and ruthless in which one can submerge one's entire identity (like the RSS [Rashtriya Swayamsevak Sangh])? Or even handing things over to a non-political institution like the army or perhaps even an alien power or a global institutional set (like the World Bank and the IMF) as is lately the wont? Each of these messiahs exploit the very disenchantment with politics and things like elections and the behaviour of politicians among the educated middle classes and, to a much smaller extent, among the masses as well.

An Unfinished Agenda Now Being Foresaken

The pity is that all such reactions to the current state of affairs turn out to be, willingly or not so willingly, detractions from the real issues facing the country and the world. They have all led to still further divides in the social fabric and often to quite volatile and bloody episodes that are presumed to provide new transitions to an alternative future based on a new theology (religious or secular) but none of which can deal with the unfinished agenda of Indian politics. At bottom this unfinished agenda is there to remove the standing shame and blot on this great nation, namely poverty and its diverse consequences, as also other items on the national agenda, some of which are real. These include the developing crisis in the relationship between diverse communities and castes, the growing regional and secessionist challenges arising out of the inability of the Indian State to respond to legitimate urges of long discriminated peoples and identities but which are increasingly treated as law and order problems, and the fast changing context of foreign policy including what may look like new opportunities in which of course we will be obliged to pay heavy costs in terms of our sovereignty as a State. These and many other 'issues' are all to a large extent related to this most basic, for long unresolved, issue of issues which, it appears in the thinking of many, to be not really resolvable and best left out of the national agenda.

It is this displacement of issues, of being gradually forced out of the focus on the real issues and getting preoccupied with a wholly different set, that is beginning to affect not just the middle class mind-set but even sections among the mass of the people. Thus, though they themselves may not be communally inclined, many of them could either be emotionally exploited or simply hijacked through the cash and criminal nexus for keeping the communal canard alive. As far as the regional and ethnic challenges to central authority are concerned, they may be to some extent an offshoot of the utter failure to provide a sense of social justice to all but, though this may be the origin of regional and ethnic upsurges, they have also acquired an autonomy and a momentum of their own, gradually moving away from the basic concern with the issues of survival, justice and poverty. From present indications it does not seem likely that we will be able to hold the country together for long except on the basis of force and there are serious limitations to how far mere force can hold a country together. Already, the Centre is increasingly giving in to demands for autonomy and special deals for different regions and sub-regions. While most of these deals are based on both the claim and the reality of regional backwardness and disparity which in turn is based on the persisting poverty of the people and their exploitation, they have acquired a life of their own and tend to detract attention from the causal nexus that lies behind them.

But the real detraction that is taking place is one that is turning attention away from domestic to foreign policy issues—getting integrated into the world economy, going in for massive loans for bailing the country out of its proven incapacity to deal with its own basic problems at home, entering into foreign strategic deals, going in for massive imports of technology of the hi-tech and nuclear variety, joining the international trade and finance regimes, signing away not just our political rights as a State but also the rights and property of our farmers and artisans through new patent laws and other trade related agreements under the auspices of GATT, and on the basis of such a changed stance on foreign affairs, hoping to emerge as the hegemonical regional power and a 'world power' of some kind. But again, as it emerges from our analysis, all of this is either meaningless for the suffering millions of India's poor or indeed further accentuates their suffering, rendering them, more than in earlier decades, dispensable. Victims of history, an unwanted people, not just for the global establishment but for the establishment at home as well. This is the true meaning of the whole paradigm of 'survival of the fittest', entailing as it does the dispensability of the 'unfit'.

Models of Development

Such a combination of proven (and in some ways admitted) incapacity to deal with basic issues and the growing insensitivity and indifference to them provides us with a fresh juncture to return to our critique of the traditional approach to these issues. The issues of poverty and destitution, of both social and regional disparities, of growing unemployment, of the considerable increase in social oppression as well as repression by agents of the State and, underlying all these, the issue of the basic model of development that we had pursued for more than four decades. And the issue of how, in pursuing such a model, we have turned our inability to deal with the core crisis facing us by coming forward with new 'crises' which have now taken hold of our minds, our policies and priorities, indeed our very thought processes and our mind-set. These are the crises of fiscal deficit, adverse Balance of Payments, slow growth of exports and dwindling reserves of foreign exchange; and all these are sought to be handled through the mind-set of liberalization, privatization and globalization.

That underlying this turn around in our perception of the nature of the 'crisis' facing us and, in a way, paving the way towards such a turn around is the general framework or 'model' of development that we had adopted to begin with is now clear. It is to the inadequacies of that model that we now turn.

As a model of development it suffers from a series of mistaken assumptions:

- The assumption that the main reason behind poverty is the inadequate supply of resources, mainly of capital resources, of enough wealth in the economy as a whole, of inadequate accumulation.
- The assumption that poverty arises out of insufficient technological growth and from a society being 'technologically backward' (the paradigm of technology being exogenous and not drawn from the traditional knowledge base of our own farming and artisan classes).
- The assumption that the disparity between the rich and the poor is basically a function of the gap between rich countries

and poor countries and that bridging that gap is only possible through international aid, increasing international trade and transfers of technology.

- The combined assumption that accumulation of capital and the creation of wealth at home and transfers of capital and technological resources from abroad will in the course of time produce a world without wants.
- The implied but not fully stated assumption that both the process of accumulation and that of technological change will not only take time but will in the meanwhile increase inequalities and call for deliberately designed depression in the condition of the masses, in particular of the rural masses, but that after these have been achieved, standards of living of the poor can be raised through State planning. In short that, unpleasant though it is, exploitation is written into the very design of development but it is exploitation of a 'structural' kind and therefore in the long run meant to benefit the poor.
- The basic assumption underlying all this that the real task is to 'expand the cake' before it can be distributed, the clear implication being that there is not much scope for redistribution while the process of accumulation and technological change is under way.

All this and many other related and subsidiary propositions represent the received wisdom of development regimes operating through the institutions of the State as well as the advocates of free market and liberalization. For, on this basic understanding there is not much difference between the two except perhaps in the sense that the 'statists' do have (or rather had) some plans of an ameliorative kind even while the gaps continued to grow and the poor continued to be marginalized from the development process. The reality is that neither the techno-economic model of accumulation nor the transfer of financial and capital resources from abroad nor for that matter the increases in trade and exports that have taken place have in any significant way affected the core of the problematique of persisting and deepening poverty.

If anything each of them have, while no doubt improving the life prospects of some strata of the population, sharpened disparities between them and the more numerous others; and, in the meanwhile, disparities between nations and regions have become still worse.

There is no hope any longer in the trickle down model of distributive justice—either within or across countries—unless it is a result of tightening the belts of the rich (again both internally and transnationally) and reducing their control over productive processes. Even the limited aim of poverty alleviation, not to speak of poverty eradication, involves reducing the riches of the rich and drastically reducing the social and economic—as well as regional—disparities through a direct attack on vested interests.

Distributive justice itself is a limited concept; it does not involve restructuring the socio-economic pyramid either within or between nations. But even this limited concept continues to be resisted by both national and international élites. Remember the unwavering stand taken by George Bush, then US President, while refusing to sign the Convention on Biodiversity. This because he could not allow the already achieved living standards of the American people (by which of course he meant the richer sections of the American people) to be in any way lowered. The same attitude applies to much of our own leadership, now increasingly tied up with the corporate sector both at home and globally. Hence the continuous whittling down of the tax burden on the rich and of subsidies for the poor, the latest manifestation of the latter being the substantial reduction of food security for those below the poverty line. There are many indications of how the old-fashioned egalitarian and 'socialistic' arguments are not only being given up but are being systematically discredited and criticized as being too ideological, anti-growth, inward-looking and pampering to the masses who are inert and inefficient and a drag on the country and its resources.

I am of course aware of the argument that taking all that the rich have and distributing it among the poor will not by itself make the condition of the poor substantially better. But this is a sheer vulgarization of the basic postulates of distributive justice which are not against accumulation, both primitive and advanced. Their critique and suggested alternative were rather with regard to the growth of inequity and injustice in spite of 'planned development' and in respect of pursuing another path to prosperity—through trickle up on the basis of planning from below and a decentralized and diverse approach to resource generation and utilization in which the poor themselves participate and put an end to their exploitation rather than through 'poverty alleviation' by relying on bureaucratic trickle down from the top to the bottom which, we know, has just not worked.

Involved in the alternative path and approach to development based on distributive justice with all its limitations is an emphasis on employment generation rather than growth *per se*, raising the purchasing power of the people and on that basis enlarging the internal market rather than expanding the export sector and drawing sustenance from the external market which, in any case, is increasingly proving a mirage. It lays special emphasis on rural development and in particular on the small and tiny sectors, drawing upon the creative capabilities and inherited skills and knowledge of artisan communities around the country who are currently being rendered unemployed in increasing numbers, and increasing involvement in the productive process of women, the migrants from rural areas and the many other social strata found in the so-called unorganized sector.

Involved in it also is a *social* policy of poverty eradication, taking full account of *cultural* prerequisites of the same, and the clear enunciation of the *politics* of development, particularly in respect of restructuring the nature of the State and its relationship to civil society. It entails a remodelling of the process and the dynamics of 'modernization'—indigenous and people-centred rather than exogenous, imported and élite dominated. The people are to be central to the whole process. But it is people who are involved in a transformative process, not just being where they are but moving forward towards a future that *they* want. Avoiding both the romanticization of the past and the romanticization of the future.

Social Dimension

I will return to the dimensions of the social policy, cultural prerequisities and the politics of transformation of the State in later chapters. At this point, there is only one aspect of social policy that I would like to stress.

We are increasingly realizing that it is only by substantial empowerment of the people, individually and culturally, that poverty can ever be removed. It cannot be removed by the bureaucracy or by the Planning Commission, no matter how well disposed a few among these institutions might be. The experience of the Planning Commission under the National Front Government (which did attempt to pursue the 'limited alternative' path spelt out above) is a grim reminder of the hopelessness of trying to do anything, however well conceived and motivated, from the top. As regards empowerment of the people, it is now clear that it is not merely a question of 'organizing the poor' as my friend the late Professor Raj Krishna, one economist who did not hesitate to think politically, used to emphasize. What is needed is *social* empowerment, enabling the people to acquire skills and capacities that are basic both to their self-respect and to their political and social standing and bargaining capacity. Massive inputs of education, health and nutrition (including public health facilities), housing and related living conditions and environmental enhancement are crucial to such empowerment. So is minimum access to land, water and common property resources.

I shall return to all this in a later chapter. The essential point right now is to note that there is a new understanding that has emerged even in respect of pursuing planned development, that it is not any longer a mere function of capital-output ratios and the like, that it is not a mere economic and technological striving, that if the goal of 'development' is to promote justice and reduce disparities and basic poverty, then the essential task is to allocate not just investible resources among firms and projects but *power* among social groups and communities. And, in order to ensure that such an allocation of power is not hijacked by privileged groups but empowers the people at large, and particularly the poor and the discriminated among them, it is essential to equip them *socially*, through the spread of education and health and housing and control over natural resources. Hence the growing realization of the critical role of investing in the 'social sectors' which happen to receive less and less attention in the march of economic rationality and in the compulsive preoccupation with fiscal deficits, export promotion and slashing of 'government expenditure' which means less and less expenditure on social sectors. It is not just a matter of what immediate compulsions are accepted by planners and politicians, nor merely a matter of the nature of budget allocations that follow from them (quite often these are mere fronts put up as rationalizations by vested interests) but what understanding informs the thinking of those in authority when it comes to the condition of the poor and oppressed sections of society, and whether there exists any real understanding of that. This includes the understanding of the NGOs who claim to identify with the poor but many of whom operate from up there and are increasingly becoming agents and allies of the establishment. Neither the government bureaucracy nor the NGO bureaucracy, neither the elected politicians nor the politicians of the so-called voluntary sector, can help remove poverty. Only when the poor themselves get engaged in that task, can poverty be removed. For this they of course need to be organized. But they also need to be empowered. Empowered socially.

Increased attention to the social dimension is not to be seen as mere advocacy for greater plan allocations and budgetary outlays to 'social sectors'. Much more than this is involved. We are aware how even the present levels of allocations have been systematically used in favour of the privileged instead of the underprivileged. Also, demands like 'raising levels of education' should not necessarily mean endorsing present approaches to education, whether primary, adult, vocational or higher. As also with health and housing. Mere increases in allocations could well lead to the further widening of gaps. What is needed are new models and methods for achieving an alternative model of society that will be people-based and people-directed. And in which people should not be confused with those in power. Or those that are known to the people in power. We should also guard against populism of all kinds, including that voiced in the name of the 'people'.

All this is, of course, by way of countering present thinking. And clearly distancing ourselves from the existing thinking and policies. It is also, at bottom, based on the realization that both the present model of development and planning, and the supposedly 'alternative' model of liberalization through privatization work against the interests of the poor. All macro-dimensional approaches and policy packages, plan schemes and legislative programmes undertaken by national governments as well as international strategies of aid and trade and transfers amount to circulation within national and international élites, and as these élites are increasingly part of the 'global reach' of transnational capital, circulation among the rich. There are also technical reasons, quite apart from social motivations, why this should be so.

Two of these may be mentioned here. One is regarding modes of transfer (capital, finance, technology) and the other with regard to the capacity to absorb for which also only the upper social strata are equipped. If anything, more recent shifts in policy and priorities are destined to further increase the power and reach of the rich at the expense of the poor. We have entered an era of *distributive injustice*. Both globalization and 'structural adjustment' under IMF and World Bank and the various budgets and other fiscal measures that are being rammed down our throats under the pressure of global institutions will do precisely this, namely push the poor towards destitution, further impoverishment and dispensability.

The Vision Underlying a New World Order

As I had laid out the emerging global design at some length in my *State Against Democracy* (Delhi: Ajanta, 1988), it is increasingly being felt in the board rooms of the 'new world order' that not only large chunks of the human population, in all societies including the hitherto affluent ones but particularly those in the Third World and even entire communities, regions and nation states are proving an unacceptable burden on the world economy. And as these segments are incapable and unwilling to mend their ways and are proving to be parasitical, their very existence will generate pressures that will gravely endanger the health and future of the world economy, and the security of the élites and 'productive classes' of the world. They must, therefore, be left to fend for themselves. To the extent that they are likely to protest and create turbulence, they should be put down ruthlessly through the development of a global strategic doctrine to which all national élites seeking entry into the world market should be made to subscribe.

The same thinking and mind-set is increasingly at work closer home too. Thus efforts towards special deals for the disinherited sections of society (SC, ST, the backwards, minorities, women and children) are likely to produce a growing backlash from the propertied classes, from sections of the 'majority', from men (when it comes to special rights for women and even for children), and generally from entrenched élites (bureaucrats in particular, party politicians in office, managers, large sections of professionals, media persons and intellectuals). It is clear now that the Mandal Commission report has so far proved to be a non-starter except in the basic sense of raising consciousness among the Dalits and other deprived communities. This, in the course of time, may lead to the mobilization of the poor and a determination to wage struggles against the system. In the long run this can lead to structural transformation. But in the shorter run it will invite both ridicule and terror. There will also be efforts to divide the poorer sections on caste, communal, religious as well as various sectarian and seemingly ideological grounds.

The ongoing erosion of the State and its key institutions alongside its decline in both accountability and providing minimum protection to the weak and the vulnerable that had already taken place during the whole decade of 1980s, is bound to further push the poor and exploited sections towards new thresholds of misery, starvation and a total sense of hopelessness (women and children being the worst victims of this) while psychologically preparing the élite towards the praxis of treating the poor as unwanted and disposable. With all this the problem of poverty will be, in this short run anyway, given the go-by. All that will be left for increasing numbers of the poor is for the men to take to crime, the women to prostitution, the children to be put on sale, and for all of them to sell the various limbs and physical organs of their bodies for cash.

The 'Lost Decade' of the Eighties

It is against this fast emerging background of erosion of norms and 'checks and balances' in the functioning of the State—and of the erstwhile state system—that we need to take stock of the period we have been through and the one we are entering. The decade of the Eighties, following the successive failures during the Seventies of populist politics ('Garibi Hatao'), the attempt at creating a 'hard State' that would remove all roadblocks and institutional obstacles and 'deliver the goods' to the people through discipline and determination (the period of Emergency) and the Janata interlude of providing an alternative to the dominant Congress culture, produced a rapid turn around in the arrangements of the State, its aims and its relationship to society at large. The 'new generation' that emerged and for a while took the country—especially its middle class and the media—by storm, gave rise to completely new modes of development and social change based on the promise of taking the country out of its stagnation and backwardness and quickly enabling it to catch up with the modern industrial world. Many were taken in by this crazy set of ideas and leaders, by 'boys' that were supposed to make the country suddenly great and powerful, led by the Big Boy who looked (not only to educated Indians but to so many foreigners too) smart, handsome, fair, modern and, as some Americans journalists and diplomats put it, 'so much like us'.

The turn around from a slow-moving, stable, moderate and more inward-looking and rooted than outward-looking and 'dynamic' polity and civilization was indeed dramatic. It was an attempt, wilful and arrogant but immensely self-confident, to leave the India we had known behind. It was a craze for power and affluence, a period of presumed progress towards a technologically dynamic and prosperous society primarily based on the cult of acquisition—of power, of ill-begotten wealth, of lifestyles based on unbecoming and vulgar consumption. With the Eighties we became a consumer society, gave rise to a consumer class, adopted the model of high technology, high communication and ultra modernization, keen to hitch our wagon to the crypto-capitalism of the maldeveloped West. But not having had the time and institutional balances and external buffers that the West had, our élite lost its sense of balance as well as its sense of history and culture and its responsibility to the large masses of the people. Underlying the new model was a certain ruthlessness and decline of values, of sensitivity, of compassion, and the entering of a kind of moral vacuum. And yet such apparent hardness of the heart was more a sign of fragility than of strength and true confidence among the élite. The fact that during this very decade the country fell prey to external dependencies in so many ways is now clear for everyone to see. The unseemly profligacy of the consumer class and the ruling élite led to incredible leaps towards a debt trap and reduced the rulers to a set of beggars who began roaming around looking for help in being bailed out of their own excesses, still legitimizing it all through the slogans of integration, globalization and 'free market'.

The political cost paid for such a combination of profligacy at home and submission to external forces abroad has been quite serious. It has meant a faster decline of every form of accountability, of integrity, of honesty in managing the affairs of society. It has meant a rather quick collapse of the basic institutions of the State, the rise of crass acquisitiveness and blunder (the much bemoaned 'Scam' of 1992 being an inevitable outcome of this). It is with this combination of a deep moral vacuum and a sharp decline in the role of the State and all the institutions of the 'system' that we had once set out tò build and had to some extent succeeded in doing, that the decade of the 1990s and those to follow will have to deal. Unfortunately, the existential crisis in which the so-called 'high growth' Eighties has landed us is not limited to the middle class. The condition of large segments of the masses is also closely linked with our inability to deal with the deep travails and traumas resulting from the flight from reality of the so-called new generation of leadership.

Legacy for the Nineties

What is now being proposed, as a result of the situation handed down by the thinking that took charge of the Eighties, is that all our problems can be solved if we are able to adopt a global perspective, not just in respect of handling the immediate consequences of the madness of the Eighties, namely the BoP crisis and the servicing of our ever growing debt, but even in respect of basic tasks like dealing with the phenomena of poverty, unemployment, inflation and ecological degradation. To what extent can one rely on such a recipe? Have we not had enough experience of the relationship between external aid and poverty alleviation? Are we not aware of the considerable experience of so many Third World countries who have already gone through the recipe being proposed to us now? Is it that poverty is what makes nations go for foreign assistance or is it rather that foreign assistance renders them perenially poor and hence still more dependent on still more assistance? Is it not true that such assistance creates a special class of beneficiaries? And what about the new framework of external assistance which we have now gone for, namely one of privatization through globalization (not just an increased role of the private sector at home)? Will not the basic consequences of this not just make us targets of the global corporate nexus, in the process forcing us to accept a whole lot of highly corrosive conditionalities, but also push us still deeper into a debt trap and to a level of external dependence from which it will be difficult for us to retract and for any future government to reverse the trend? And, more than all this, deal a deadly blow to the poor and the working class and our democratic structure?

The Debt Trap

The full implications of the debt trap in which more and more of the Third World countries are caught (including those for whom the IMF is working out all kinds of 'solutions') are not yet clear. But a few things are clear: wherever they have gone too far in that direction, nations in debt have been forced to go for a restructuring of their international balance of forces, both socio-economically and politically. This has happened even where formal 'democracy' has been accepted by the élite or imposed by Western powers. They have had to indulge in a rape of the countryside and expose it to monopolistic global forces. The craze for consumer goods, the growth in hi-fi tourism, the brainwashing of the highly educated that ends up in their wanting to migrate to foreign lands, the increasing dependence on local leasing and hire purchase companies for 'keeping up with the Joneses' in respect of consumerism, which only means getting more and more in debt at home while the country gets more and more in debt externally, the growth of a whole banking sector given more and more to the servicing of debts, all this results in the nation as a whole becoming increasingly unable to regain its economic autonomy and hence also unable to withstand external political pressures.

The Dunkel Draft

On top of this have come the compulsions brought by GATT and the Dunkel Draft which, in the name of freeing trade and opening up access to technology, will in fact draw nations like ours into a global monopoly trap (alongside the debt trap) and do this through new legal devices with which we will be forced to fall in line. Here too, though the way the draft and the proposed treaty on Intellectual Property Rights is presented gives the impression of being limited to industrial items and pharmaceuticals, in fact the worst attack will be on the countryside and agriculture and on basic biological and genetic resources including our large repertoire of seeds, in the final analysis, our real wealth lying in our earth's womb which we always thought nobody could trample upon. And the worst hit sections will be the rural, the tribal, the forest folk, the landless and the poor, and above all the women.

Coming back to the travails and traumas produced by the new policies of the Eighties, it is not just the poor and economically dispossessed that have been affected and will be affected in the years to come, and to which will be added a new genre of 'oustees', including those currently holding secure positions in both the public and the private sectors; many others will be affected too, particularly, those who will be pushed out culturally (out of their diverse social and community settings and their various highly skilled vocations like the weavers and the artisans and the indigenous artists), psychologically (through the immense dislocations that the turn around described above will produce) and physically (their number exceeding the many millions already present of physically disabled and medically neglected strata, especially in the rural areas, to which can be added the physical as well as the emotional shocks to which increasing numbers of women are being subjected). The problem of poverty is more all encompassing than what happens to the 'poor' as statistically defined.

The Emerging Profile of Poverty

Poverty is seen, in the historical period in which we find ourselves, to be a product of a *system of deprivation and insecurity*. In this it is not just that the poor are pitched against the rich and the rich against the poor. The poor also fight against other poor, faced as they all are by an overall climate of deprivation and a growing sense of insecurity among various sub-sections of them. But such a combination of deprivation and sense of insecurity—getting worse due to inflation and unemployment—is also hurting the less poor sections of society. It is producing divisions among the middle classes and even sections of the rich. And they remain divisions even though they may be less violent and harsh than the ones that divide the poor; and more ideological than reality-induced, the reality being the intense pressure to catch up with sections of the upper class and rich.

Even more basic than this cultural syndrome of poverty is yet another fact. The modernist thinking that economic growth will create wealth and this will in turn 'trickle down' does not take account of the wealth that had already existed through long periods of history and that is now being destroyed in the process of creating new wealth (agricultural land, forests and common property resources as against goods that are manufactured at large and the food that comes to the mandi that is then measured in Gross Domestic Product [GDP] terms). It is the same with what is proposed under GATT and the Dunkel draft—we are already slowly eating away the capital created over centuries by our forebears which, it is now discovered, is being depleted at a much faster rate and which can perhaps never be replenished. The whole ecological dimension of what causes poverty in the first place, then sustains and later on accentuates it is not even touched upon by those who offer 'global' solutions to us. In fact there may be an inherent contradiction between ecological and economic considerations once we move into the global space and give up our own spaces.

It is the whole issue of endogenity versus exogenity and its import for the incidence of poverty. It is my position, which I will take up in greater detail in the chapter 'Environment and Poverty', that both the causes of poverty (as a characteristic of a social system) and the solutions of poverty that are being offered (as part of the economic package) cannot be dealt with without reference to both natural and human resources, skills and technologies which are already there in plenty and can make a vital contribution to the fulfilment of basic needs and human rights but which are presently endangered and can be undermined very fast. I am not an environmental fundamentalist and do believe in the need to creatively combine tradition and modernity but I cannot at the same time ignore the considerable drainage of natural resources and endowments that has been caused by the modern conception of development and which threatens to prove more damaging and defenceless under the onslaught of globalization.

Having said all this and given all my apprehensions, I do not think that the recipe of development through globalization and integration into the world supermarket being offered by the World Bank and the IMF will succeed. Indian society and polity cannot be so easily 'integrated' nor even, for that matter, the Indian economy. So much of it is both outside the world market and outside the organized economy, as well as outside the sway of the State that is now sought to be colonized. The problem is not that all these people may succeed in carrying out their distorted vision and make the country surrender to invading interests by getting integrated into their monolithic enterprise. There is no fundamental threat to our sovereignty, at any rate not our sovereignty as a people (it is the sovereignty of the Indian State that seems more vulnerable). The problem is rather what damage the sheer *attempt* to integrate will do to the country, its institutions and its people. From what we have already seen, this damage is not restricted to the economic dimensions of poverty but goes far beyond, affecting the psychological and civilizational springs of our beings.

It is in this respect that, having provided an overview of the basic problem of poverty, I would now like to turn to its social, ecological, cultural and ethical dimensions.

Cultural Terrain

We have come to a stage in this essay when it becomes necessary to delve deeper into the poverty syndrome that has emerged as a result of the model of development that was adopted, the kind of State that this model first engendered and then undermined, and the consequences of both for the survival and sustenance of peoples and communities. As already stressed in the analysis provided so far, the poverty syndrome in contemporary Indian and Third World contexts involves our having to probe beyond 'poverty' as it has been traditionally understood. It takes us into the terrain of inhumanity, violence, criminality, corruption of the moral fibre of society and the resulting destruction of a pluralist culture of communities and world-views. It brings us face to face with a certain tearing apart caused by new schisms which may be based on material conditions to begin with but have subsequently produced deep animosities, ill-will and ill-feeling between groups and communities, often verging on contempt and hatred for the 'other', threatening the age-old cohesion, sense of composure and feelings of co-existence that have characterized this land.

As I argued in the last chapter, Indian culture and 'civil society' are not equipped to handle the new types of disparities occasioned by the modern phenomenon of poverty; they have handled disparities and inequalities for long but these were endogenous to their own structure and hierarchy. Similarly, Indian society has handled violence and strife of various kinds but the violence that it now has to deal with is of a totally different kind, far more confrontationist and zero-sum, leaving little scope for negotiating one's course towards a way out. (This has not only happened in local settings, e.g., what happened in Bombay in January 1993, but also where macro problems are concerned both of a regional kind, e.g., Punjab and Kashmir and Tamil Nadu, and of a social kind, e.g.,

Mandal). It is strife that cannot be brought under control through either the traditional mechanisms of civil society or through the institutions of the modern State. In recent times civil society had, given its own erosion and failure to handle new kinds of crises, increasingly been relying on the State and considered it to be the main bulwark against divisive forces. But this understanding of the role of modern institutions in handling the new traumas and crises engulfing a traditional society has obviously not stood the test of time. As the State has also failed in dealing with poverty itself, in some ways the cause of these other traumas, it becomes far more difficult to deal with the overall problem.

What is Poverty?

In order to dwell further on these deeper kinds of terrain of the poverty syndrome, it may be useful to raise a few critical conceptual questions so as to proceed with some clarity and be able to comprehend better the overall problem. Even on the simple problem of poverty in the economic sense, there is need for more clarity than there seems to be at present. Is poverty in a given society a mere absence of affluence or prosperity or general well-being, a mere lack of something that society designates as desirable and worth having? And for an individual or a group, does moving out of poverty mean simply catching up with the rich? As for the policy-makers, is reducing the 'gap' between rich and poor merely a matter of crossing the 'poverty line'? Or, on the opposite side of thinking about poverty, are the poor mere discards of society, the 'dispossessed'—dispossessed of their own resources and institutions—and since excluded, in which society, out of design as it were, moves on without them, leaving them behind, finding them of no use, in fact considering them a burden and an obstacle in the way of 'progress' and 'development'. In this latter case the goal of development is no longer removing—or reducing—poverty but of moving ahead with those who have either already made it or appear to have a good chance of making it, of extending the frontiers of science and technology to those who can absorb them, making society more 'modern', more 'competitive' internationally and more 'equal' to others with whom one would like to move on, by definition without the poor, either of one's own society or the poor at large. And then the crucial question: In the latter way of thinking, is not poverty a result of development rather than a cause for undertaking it? Is it not a function that deprivation and oppression inherent in the development process, always happen to people who are rendered poor?

Is poverty a necessarily relative thing or are there measurable attributes which by themselves describe a person or a country as being poor?

Is poverty a function of inequality? But then how is it that there is greater equality among the poor and greater gaps and inequalities among the rich (even if the latter as a group be 'co-equal')? For if poor countries are said to be characterized by 'extremes of inequality', is it not also true that the richer countries have still greater inequality between those at the top of the economic pyramid and those at the bottom? In any case, is there any sense in measuring the gap between extremes?

And in what sense do you use terms like 'poor country' and 'rich country'—how do macro categories (country, society, nation) derive their economic standing in some international listing (confining ourselves for the moment to Economics)? Or is it rather that the goal is to create a prosperous *country* rather than eradicate the persistence of poverty among the *people*, in a way perhaps even ignoring the very existence of the poor? (Herein lies the real dichotomy in thinking.)

What is the relationship between poverty and injustice? And what should be a primary social goal: justice or equality? Isn't the latter—progressive and 'socialistic' though it sounds—liable to straitjacket all and render them subjects of a benevolent State, quite apart from its inherent competitiveness and mechanistic ethics (and the tension and violence generated by the same)?

There is also the question of the relationship between poverty and access to power, the whole issue of poverty and *disempowerment*, how poverty becomes a basis of exclusion from the system, a theme touched upon earlier. Of defining poverty in terms of being pushed out of the margins of tolerance. Of conceiving poverty itself as a mode of oppression both by the State and by civil society. Ordinarily oppression and poverty can be considered separate and distinct phenomena but they have in the contemporary global context been found to be part of a single phenomenon.

And then of course all this has to be thought of as part of a broader cultural pattern in which not just the poor but almost everyone is being reduced to an atom which is then encapsulated in a prison house, be it development, the State or (now) the Market. Basic to it is a condition of being disembodied, torn apart from both primary structures of family and community and secondary associations like the trade union, the voluntary association, the party and the State as well. The poverty of the poor becomes part of the cultural poverty of all. But it is a condition that hits those hardest that are materially and physically poor and deprived as they are not only excluded from the so-called 'fruits of development' but also from the community and the social structure, the environment and the natural resource base, the whole system of obligations and belonging on which they had traditionally depended for their identity, and now from the State as well which was supposed to provide a new and liberating foothold for the weak and the traditionally oppressed.

Seen in this way, there are two opposite positionings of the poor, the movement from the one to the other constituting present reality. The first of these—poverty as a social construct—is a description of the way society is structured, in which being poor and living at subsistence levels in a condition of extreme frugality can be either elevating and a source of pride and exemplary behaviour or humiliating if caused by attitudes of deliberate distancing and segregation by civil society, but in either case contained within the given social space. The second is poverty as a condition in which a large number of *individuals* are found (they have already moved out of the community nexus) as a function of exclusion, abandonment and disenfranchisement. The current situation is one in which poverty as a social construct has moved from the first positioning to the second. (An important caveat can be entered here. Paradoxical though it may sound, is it not true that it is only the latter position that lends itself to interventionist policies and mobilizational strategies, of course producing the costs inherent in being 'mobilized', giving rise to a populist politics and a populist 'mass' culture, with serious consequences for the future of democracy?)

Today the social construct of poverty is fast becoming a *global* construct, a universal phenomenon with universal solutions offered by global institutions which claim to possess a universal mandate. Under their aegis poverty removal is also becoming a *futuristic* construct in which the past and the experience of the past must be left behind as, we are told, there can be no going back, only moving ahead into the mythical twenty-first century. The earlier packages of assistance and aid from 'external' and 'foreign' (not 'global') sources are giving place to global transfers of technology, capital and patents, but more important than all that, a global transfer of ideas and ideology, a paradigm of thought, a culture of thinking and extending and diffusing that thinking to permeate all societies. It is a construct that goes far beyond the rather limited 'neo-colonial' design of the Truman Doctrine and the many other constructs of 'development co-operation' that followed, including the various UN development decades. The entire thinking of helping the poor through international effort has thus undergone a sea change—from the premise of humanitarianism and an effort to deal with a diversity of human situations to that of technology and a homogenous package for all societies.

The Notion of Rights

Similarly, the notion of 'Rights' through which the poor are supposed to acquire new capabilities within the system and under the patronage of the State has, in an increasingly competitive and consumer society that also promotes the cult of equality and levelling of all human beings to a standardized set, led to a situation in which everyone has been asked to join the same rat race. As theoretically all are equal and all have access to the same rights and as society is committed to achieve the goals of prosperity and affluence, the poor should have no hesitation or compunction in joining that race. The reality, of course, is that given the *structure* in which the poor are positioned, such a rat race only reduces them to a position of rats who are then led out of mainstream economy by the latest version of a pied piper in the form of the international (as well as national) technocrat. In the meanwhile, specific rights that had already been achieved and special programmes worked out for them by the Planning Commission and various other bodies, such as the rights to education, health, shelter, cheap transport and healthy environment are all being steadily run down, under the same new 'global village' that the poor are being beckoned to inhabit. The rights that are now being offered are based not on real but induced needs, induced by the MNCs, the corporate mass media, the commercial ad agencies and even the new-style NGOs that are being prompted to join the new bandwagon of development through structural adjustment and globalization.

This new approach to rights also covers and includes areas like environment, health, education, 'women's rights', new opportunities for the youth—all of them packaged within the framework of the new model of transnational growth and development. Environment becomes 'management of resources', health leads to more and more imports of drugs and acceptance of patents on them by the MNCs, education means more and more avenues for middle class kids to go abroad, women's rights get more and more internationalized through conferences and research projects while the rights of the youth get translated increasingly in yuppie terms, much of the action and the excitement of the new hedonism being largely limited to the urban middle class though having seductive value for the young among the poor too. Such a pursuit of rights as well as the global promotion of 'human rights' through the establishment of multi-party systems have created a growing feeling that the post-Cold War era is leading to a more liberal society alongside a liberalized economy. But the sad reality is that whether it is the former Soviet Union and other socialist countries or certain Latin American and Asian countries, the 'democracy revolution' is only reinforcing the prevailing structures of domination, exploitation and violence with the poor, who have been deprived of their community roots as well as the spaces that had been created for them by the State in earlier decades. They have not only been deprived of their real basic rights but have also been reduced to a diffuse and impersonal and malleable mass precisely as a result of the advent of the new package of rights for them.

In India there was, in recent years, an effort to create a new agenda of planning and development based on quite a different conception of rights—the right to work, the right to information, the right to guaranteed access to the Public Distribution System (the PDS), the right to a minimum package for women and children, but also rights based on certain social priorities, for e.g., the reservation of special spheres of economic activity for the small scale, village and tiny sectors, and of course the political rights inherent in the model of a federal and decentralized scheme of governance. This agenda seems to have now been given up as the trend is increasingly from decentralization to globalization and from discretionary schemes meant for the poor and the marginalized sections to generalized patterns of growth in which the emphasis will be on rates of growth and modes of financing that growth. Part of the agenda that was tried out earlier (in parts during the Second to the Fourth Plan periods and in a more focused way during the National Front government and in the first model of the Eighth Plan called 'Towards Social Transformation') involved a major effort at redistributive justice. The thinking behind such an effort was one of restricting and containing the vast and growing and fattening spaces pre-empted by the rich and super-rich, the vulgar consuming class of the *nouveau riche* and the class of smugglers and hoarders and dealers in black money. This too is not any longer being pursued. If anything, the levels of taxation on the rich have been brought down, subsidies for the poor have been slashed, institutional opportunities for agricultural labour and women in rural areas have been drastically reduced. In such a condition in which government has given up its constitutional role and is, under pressure from IMF, the World Bank and GATT, coming down heavily on the poor and the unemployed—and also employing brutal methods against those who take up the cause of the poor—the 'struggle for rights' becomes all the more crucial. But, it will have to be based on a conception of rights that is wholly different from the one propagated globally.

Decolonizing the Poor

These various dimensions take us to terrains of the poverty syndrome that are different from the traditional economic framework of dealing with poverty. That framework depended largely on bureaucratic targeting and centralized schemes that were to be implemented through a machinery of government that had continued to be colonial. The frustration with that model led to a greater reaction from the right than the left, producing the model of privatization and globalization. I have argued at length how this reaction, far from improving matters, will only worsen them, particularly from the point of view of the poor. But if we consider the problem of poverty in larger and comprehensive cultural terms and if we go beyond a mere analysis of economic exploitation and growing inequality and see how the poor have been deprived and excluded from the cultural sphere itself, we will need to admit that even in our earlier efforts after independence to build a just and humane society, we had failed to develop a model for the decolonization of the poor. Given the fact that the worst colonization that modern society has produced is not colonization of territories and nations but that of the people, we failed to develop the ideology, the values and above all the institutions through which the poor will cease to be subjects and become citizens.

It is this failure that lies behind the increasing alienation of and from the poor, a sense that they don't matter (both in their eyes and in our eyes), also that it doesn't really matter who is in power. It is this deeper psychic condition that defines the cultural context of poverty. Even where economic poverty has been handled to some extent, poverty in the other kinds of terrain still persists, in fact becomes more preponderant. This then replays the economic scenario of poverty too. For, basically, without the deeper cultural base, it is not possible to achieve human well-being. Even if it is temporarily brought about through some administrative or technological means, or in some special area or region, or for a set of individuals who are fortunately placed, it will soon disappear. To be real, well-being has to be of communities, of the larger society, of the whole culture. Well-being merely of individuals, of a randomized set thereof, will only produce further alienation and create an insecure basis for survival.

Social Poverty

In sum, what is neglected in the prevailing approach to poverty is the *social* dimension thereof, that the poor—as poor—are a social class, not just an economic or statistical category. Even if economic or financial inputs are provided, several sections of the poor could continue to be socially backward, underprivileged, discriminated against, perceived as backward by society at large, and as a result of this, oppressed in many ways. The sweeper and the carrier of night soil make money all right but he or she does not cease to be poor. Particularly in a society like ours, the phenomenon of *social poverty* (as distinct from economic poverty) needs to be fully comprehended if we are to get out of the vicious cycle of poverty-development-poverty. Similarly, individuals or communities who are simply dispossessed of the resources (mostly natural) they had or at least had access to and are forcibly displaced or compelled to migrate, then rendered homeless in the cities and compelled to 'survive' in the straitjacket of the urban marketplace, even if 'compensated' by more income than before, do not cease to be poor. What you have here, alongside social poverty is *ecological poverty*, which again, if not fully comprehended, will reinforce the cycle of development-poverty-development. Indeed, the only avenues possible for such socially and ecologically dispossessed are economic and financial, including the lowly and humiliating 'jobs' in the informal sector, as also through the economic avenues provided by crime and organized violence on this or that group or community (perhaps the largest 'rate of growth' is to be found in this sector). But none of these avenues really enable the poor to cease to be poor. Poverty unless it is made a direct focus of public policy, as argued in an earlier chapter, takes such a variety of forms that it becomes almost impossible to remove from the social fabric.

Particularly serious is the condition of those who have been forcibly *physically* dislocated and uprooted, dishinherited of both space and livelihood and then thrown into a vortex of slums and ghettos from which the only 'exit' point is crime and terrorism and social militancy through wielding weapons of violence, the gun-toting youth that abounds in our cities and even small towns. Taking place here is not just criminalization of the poor because of their condition of poverty but rather rendering people who were not poor, like the tribals who have been forced out of their habitats and cultural inheritance wherever large dams like Narmada or Tehri have been built, into becoming poor and *then* forced to participate in criminal or para-criminal activities.

Growing Volatility

But the cultural terrain of poverty is found along other dimensions too. Quite apart from analysing the way the issue of poverty itself acquires a cultural terrain—the transition from a social construct that is endogenous to one's own society to a global construct laid out by an exogenous model; from a conception of rights based on fulfilment of basic needs to one based on inducements of a globalized consumer society; from a view of democracy based on a federal and decentralized structure of the State to one based on a centralized and globalized notion of 'human rights'—there is need to delve into other manifestations, arising out of the basic condition of poverty, in the same terrain.

The 'boiling conundrum' that we spoke of in an earlier chapter gets expressed in the growing volatility arising from rendering large sections of society unwanted and dispensable, the tensions within the middle class as a result of the new policies, the erosion of accountability and sense of responsibility in the élite and the growing combination of helplessness and ruthlessness and amorality in the same élite. This mood of despair leading to a look-out for a new genre of 'leaders' promising protection against both the politicians and the police, all of this facilitating a completely new agenda for Indian politics, society and culture.

Central to this agenda—and the general social and political process that is unfolding—is the spread of communal identities and demands, backed increasingly by religious dogma and fanaticism that is directed against other communities. All of this arises from the failure of the State in dealing with basic social issues, the growing alienation of people from the mainstream and the vacuum created by the erosion of institutions, playing into the hands of the new militancies of Right Reaction.

Right Reaction

The phenomenon of Right Reaction has, of course, a national as well as a global dimension: it is communalism and religious bigotry at home and colonization (rather, recolonization) engendered by world capitalism, globally. What we are currently going through is a completely new convergence of the domestic right and the global right, of the excesses of cultural communalism and the excesses of economic secularism. It is thus interesting that the new-style Bharatiya Janata Party (BJP) supports both the economic package of colonization and the social package of communalism. Through such a convergence it offers a really 'New Agenda'. Needless to say, for people at large, particularly for the poor, for the social (as against religious) minorities, such an agenda represents a major detraction from real issues. (As for the religious minorities, apart from the short-sighted and fanatic among them, it is more than mere detraction; it is an agenda of near disaster.)

Hindutva

Arising out of the spread of the communal ethos (which has been with us for quite some time now and was started by the Congress Party itself) is the Hindutva neurosis based on the proposition that the Indian State and the economic development process have benefited the minorities and discriminated against the majority Hindus and that this has been possible because the Hindus are divided as a result of so much diversity and therefore need to be brought together under one homogeneous identity which could then rule the country and 'put the minorities in their place'. That such a doctrine and ideology represent a collective neurosis will be clear to anyone who has a sense of the basic cultural grounding of the Indian people. It is not only turning Hinduism upside down as I have argued in several of my recent writings and as many other scholars have shown too; it is also clear that what is being proposed in the name of Hindu society as a whole is really the interest of upper caste Hindus as opposed to the SCs, STs and backward classes. What is more, such an ideology will cause immense cultural damage to Indian society as a whole, Hindu society being at the core of it. India *sans* pluralism and diversity will cease to be India. It will cease to be a civil society. And as pluralism gives way, the social structure of care and compassion for the weak and the deprived will give way too: the positive political dimensions of caste and caste identities (especially for the Dalits and the backward castes) will be replaced by an apolitical, macho and unicultural imposition of so-called 'religion'.

But it is not just the social costs of Hindutva that one feels concerned about. It is also the political cost of the same, including those for the very leaders who are promoting this new-fangled ideology. For, once the model of religious chauvinism and the new cults of fundamentalism and communal violence slip, the whole initiative for running the country and interpreting the Constitution will pass to irredentist and obscurantist elements—after 6 December 1992 it was the 'kar sevaks' on the one hand and the 'sadhus' on the other. While the precise constituents of the religious bandwagon may shift, these two basic types—lumpens on the one hand and priests on the other—will remain. As for the cult of communal violence, it is likely to merge into the larger more organic cult of violence and take it to new plateaus of vehemence and ferocity, aimed to begin with against just the religious minorities, especially the Muslims, but in the long run against the weak and deprived and poor of all communities. The joining of anti-reservationist and anti-Muslim mobs in Gujarat during the anti-reservation riots of 1985 provides the classic case. After Ayodhya, this combination of communal feelings and violence against the lower castes of the Hindus and Muslims is likely to spread because of Hindutva. But more important than this is the fact that even the leaders of communal organizations like the BJP and the Vishwa Hindu Parishad (VHP) will lose control over the lumpens and the sadhus, resulting in a breakdown of institutional norms and the much-advertised 'discipline'.

The sequence that emerges, then, is first the marginalization of secular parties and the emergence of a communal party and then within the communal party the marginalization of the relatively 'secular' leadership of the party by fanatics on the one hand and the 'mob' on the other. As the sequence progresses, the concern for the lower classes recedes more and more. With this, Brahminism will emerge with full vengeance.

Xenophobia

The communal backlash and the atmosphere of hatred and animus against all kinds of minorities that this will create will also have other consequences (some of which have already started). For instance, there is a growing feeling of revulsion against immigrants, refugees and other 'outsiders'. Together with the backlash against religious minorities like the Muslims, this will produce the scenario of 'ethnic cleansing', somewhat like that which has taken place in Bosnia: genocidal acts at bottom in which first a set of trained cadres and then, unfortunately owing to the growth of fanaticism even among the otherwise oppressed and alienated strata, entire communities may get drawn. In our case, such xenophobia is accentuated by the growing competition produced by ever deepening states of poverty and unemployment and gets targeted against the 'outsider'. This too has been long in the making as has communalism. The 'sons of soil' movement was spearheaded by the Shiv Sena in Bombay, the same Sena that partly organized the planned killings of Muslims in Bombay in January 1993, again forcing large numbers of them to leave Bombay and to clear the slums and other habitats occupied by the working class so that the slum lords could resume their designs for land grab which they had always wanted to. That the slum lords partly financed the Shiv Sena and the mass killings of Muslims should come as no surprise.

Role of the State

If we bring together the various ingredients of the cultural backlash against the poor—the economic poor, the social poor, the ecological poor and the poor as minorities—that have been discussed in this chapter, the question arises: where do the poor turn in such a situation—one not just of deprivation along a single dimension but of deprivation that is multidimensional? Our experience so far shows that the poor and the marginalized have nowhere to turn other than to the State. As we think of 'the poor and the marginalized' in terms of other social categories, e.g., the minorities, the migrants and the refugees, the displaced tribals, the victims of anti-reservation riots, again they have no other instrument to fall back on either for their physical protection or for their social status and well-being, but the State. In the long run, of course, the struggle *against* an oppressive State and *for* transformation of the State needs to be waged. But even for that there is need not to allow the erosion of legitimacy of the State or, for instance, allow sections of the people perched between the State and other institutions (like the Market or the priestly class) to tilt towards the latter. Even a State dominated by 'vested interests' could be made available at least to some extent to aggrieved people and classes unlike the Market or the priestly class. Also, the 'democratic space' that has shrunk of late can be fought for only within the institutional framework provided by the State. As has been graphically brought out by Amartya Sen, the 'long stretch of history' consisted of centuries of misery and travails, feudal atrocities and mass slavery until a series of revolts and revolutions brought into being the modern democratic state and the ideas of justice and equality.

It would be sheer blindness to ignore this lesson of contemporary history, that it was in the public arena and mainly through the instrumentality of the State that the clash of interests could be made to favour the struggling and labouring classes (organized and unorganized). Whether it is a question of removing poverty economically by creating employment and purchasing power in the rural hinterlands or it is liberation from the social and cultural terrain of poverty, history summons us to work out a long run partnership between the poor and the modern State. Such a partnership calls for both transformation of the State and a transformation in our thinking about poverty. The Indian State which has been defaulting for too long on its basic commitments to the people of India has not only to be brought back to resume the mandate bequeathed to it by history, it has also to be provided with new roots as indicated by the contemporary stirrings of Indian society and culture. These include the struggles of the poor peasantry which has borne the brunt of economic exploitation and social ostracism, the regional movements for recreating the country's confederal history which is its real history, the seething revolts of class and caste from the erstwhile peripheries and backwaters of Hindu society that are now coming alive and, through each of these, relocating the challenge of poverty by expanding its cultural terrain. In this lies the basic cultural call of our time. For both the Indian State and the Indian people.

Environment and Poverty

The environmental dimension of the poverty issue has been touched upon indirectly earlier, at various places; there is need to consider it directly. Despite a lot of discussion and assertions with regard to prioritizing one or the other—poverty being the greatest pollutant or, at the other extreme, 'development' being the greatest cause of environmental erosion—there seems to be no real clarity on the precise relationship between the two. Needless to say, a given model of development can give rise to erosions of both types, to large disparities and imbalances and erosions of living conditions all round—and consequent poverty—and to environmental degradation and destruction. Examples that are often given of the latter are destruction of forest and water resources, the growing incidence of famines and floods, as also of desertification. Examples of the former are in the form of malnutrition, hunger and starvation—the obvious indicators of poverty. Also mentioned are the displacement of communities that had been environmentally sustained for long, the growing brutality against minorities and migrant populations, these latter often caused in the name of development and thus not always admitted as indicators of destruction yet increasingly recognized as problem areas, even by global think tanks like the World Bank. As both these phenomena are admitted to be caused by existing patterns of development, it is also broadly recognized that there is need to move to an alternative approach to development which could simultaneously reduce poverty and arrest environmental erosion. Where things are not clear is what state of environment leads to what state of poverty and what pressures emanating from the poor produce environmental costs.

The 'Limits to Growth' Debate

There has of course been considerable debate on this issue which has given rise to opposite positions. The widely published report of the Club of Rome entitled *Limits to Growth* (New York: Basic Books, 1972) and the build-up of opinion around it led to the belief that there are inherent limits to growth that are largely ecological. At the other end of the debate are found two positions: first, that there are no such limits as modern technology posits a continuous possibility of growth and, second, that there are indeed limits to growth but these are caused by a particular model of development and consumption and that there are sufficient resources in the world to sustain the basic needs of all people and societies if only the rich and the profligate could be made to give up their luxurious and wasteful ways. A close examination of the available evidence as well as options before mankind suggests the following:

- That there are no inherent limits to growth that are ecological and 'natural'. In fact there are no limits posed by nature *qua* nature.
- That one could in fact argue the opposite, namely that growth is inherent in nature and that human interventions in nature can be both growth-inducive and ecologically sustainable.
- That primitive accumulation with which the accumulation process is supposed to begin need not be destructive or exploitative of nature. In fact, primitive accumulation can go hand in hand with 'primitive communism'. As regards the movement from this to more abstract and concentrated forms of capital accumulation, this too could either generate levels of growth and modes of development that are sustainable and conserving of natural resources or give rise to types of growth and development that generate disparities and exploitative structures. And, whether it is the one or the other depends on regimes of regulation and governance, that is to say, on the nature of the political system.
- That even in this respect there have been, historically speaking, social systems that have allowed structures of

disparity, even promoted disparity to an extent (as with the Hindus or certain types of European feudalism) but within a certain balance and containment so that at no point is anyone completely excluded or even marginalized.

- That there is something about *modernity* and the development and consumption model it has given rise to that has proved exploitative—within and across societies—and inherently inequitous and unjust, hence inherently marginalizing sections and classes of society, excluding them, and as the competitive cultural trait overpowers the co-operative and mutualist one, even killing and repressing, maiming and chaining up and destroying them. In the process, creating institutions and political systems based on both oppression and exploitation of humans (slavery, colonialism, bonded labour, untouchability, forms of patriarchy) and erosion of both nature in its pristine forms and other species and forms of life.
- That the basic challenge of ecology (or 'ecodevelopment') is that of creating political systems that set limits to the exploitation of men and women, to production systems that are based on exploitation, and to the use and abuse of nature that follow from such a model of human and social development. Ecological destruction is in the ultimate analysis politically sanctioned and organized—and institutionalized; in short, embodied in a particular model of the *State*. It does not necessarily follow that a socialist state committed to achieve equality and justice based on equality is necessarily less destructive of the environment. History seems to point in the other direction. Socialist states in the West (and by copying the West) have also been based on the logic of modernity and institutionalization of the exploitation of humans and erosion of nature. Gorbachev admitted as much in his *Perestroika*. Massive evidence from China has suggested the same even in respect of a high incidence of famines and droughts as shown in the early work of Amartya Sen who provided a comparative analysis of China and India.

There are three other issues:

- Concepts of equality and of justice based on equality are inherently competitive and zero-sum but concepts of justice do not necessarily have to be based on equality.
- The phenomenon of class in human development and of class-based society (which is then sought to be transformed through class struggle which is supposed to lead to a classless utopia) point to the same results. Inherent in this model of 'progress' are escalating forms of exploitation, strife and war, each of which has an ecological component.
- The same is the case with the role of technology. From technology as a means of equipping man to move out of states of poverty and deprivation—and 'backwardness'—to allowing it to become an end. In that lies the rise of the technocratic systems of knowledge and science, technocratic bureaucracy and the State, and technology-based patterns of *global* development including those advocating interdependence and a 'common future' (from Brandt to Bruntland, even to Nyerere, all based on aid and transfer, basically transfers of technology, the same being the case with even the advocacy in the mid-Seventies of a new international economic order). In fact the assumption that application of capital will lead to development and that it is the lack of adequate capital that is the basic problem facing the Third World is also part of the same mind-set.

As against such globalized prescriptions (though in a way contributing to it), spokesmen of the Third World—both governments and intellectuals and, lately, even 'environmentalists'—are arguing the case for the South catching up and the North paying the price for it through massive allocation of resources. The case is basically argued in terms of removal of poverty, environmental erosion itself being perceived as mainly a consequence of development policies pursued by the North, hence the need for it to compensate the South for its lag in development, curiously (even if inadvertently) wanting the South to catch up with the same development path that the North is being criticized for. This is being couched in the framework of the current debate on 'environment and development', it being argued that development is the key priority only as a part of which environmental concerns could also be pursued. From what has been said above, I do not subscribe to this statist developmentalist prescription in the name of bridging North-South disparities. Indeed, I see in it the South falling in to the trap of a global consumerist, market-oriented mind-set which then serves to promote demands for more and more capital and technology flows from the North to the South and gradually make the latter accept the model of globalization through 'integration into the world market'. This may be a good point to quickly review the diversity of positions that have been taken on the relationship between environment and poverty.

While there is a general consensus that poverty and the related problems of social injustice, low productivity and inadequate resources have been and must remain the central focus of any effort at planning or governance in India, within that broad context, five types of positions have been taken about the environment.

Differing Positions

The first is that protection of the environment is an ethical imperative, independent of concerns about poverty and development. That animals and plants have a right to life, irrespective of human needs.

This position is theoretically very strong, though not unassailable. Its serious detractors argue that the world is governed by the law of nature where predators abound and where almost every species has to fight for survival against other species, and every individual against other individuals.

They, therefore, conclude that concerns about the 'rights' of plants and animals are themselves anthropomorphic, as they reflect human ethical thinking rather than the law of nature.

They also point out the impossibility of living in 'total harmony' with nature, considering that even as we breathe, or walk, or eat, we are destroying thousands of living creatures, just as the antibodies in our systems are killing millions of bacteria and virus.

But apart from the theoretical and practical difficulties, this position is not very influential because its proponents are usually well-to-do people whose basic needs are well satisfied and who express their ethical concerns through mild sacrifices like vegetarianism.

Detractors argue that if these 'ethical' beings were to face the real deprivations of life, then perhaps their ethics would be modified.

The second position is that poverty alleviation and environmental conservation are two sides of the same coin. To alleviate poverty, one has to conserve and regenerate the environment. This has been argued most effectively for communities primarily dependent on natural resources for their subsistence, like tribals and fisherfolk, among others.

Many of the most successful grassroots environmental movements are among communities whose primary or only source of subsistence is dependent on the ecosystem which development projects or vested interests are threatening. However, efforts to expand the applicability of this argument to other communities whose linkage with nature might not be so direct, have not met with much success. Therefore, apart from tribals, fisherfolk, forest dwellers, and other such, little support for this position is seen among the rest of the country, especially among the urbanized and the 'modern'.

The third position is expressed by those who argue that unless environmental conservation is ensured, all efforts at poverty alleviation in the long term (or even medium term) would fail. These are people demanding that all development, national and global, should be environmentally sustainable.

The fourth position is that protection and regeneration of the environment is one of the means, perhaps the best, of alleviating poverty. This has been argued most effectively on behalf of agricultural and pastoral communities who benefit greatly from environmental protection, and on behalf of the millions of underemployed or unemployed rural people who could be provided sustainable employment, with very low investments, in activities related to environmental regeneration.

Finally, at the other extreme, is the position that environmental concerns are élitist, anti-development, against the poor, and should not be taken seriously in a country like India. This is a position that many Indian planners, politicians and bureaucrats hold. It is also a position which, until recently, was quite commonly held by social and political activists of all hues but green. This is also the position that needs detailed examination if the current debate on environment and development has to be understood.

Unfortunately, the economic and cultural push to move from tribal and agricultural lifestyles to urban and industrialized ones—which constitute the essence of the 'economic development' paradigm—is also a push to move from lifestyles which were fully or primarily dependent on natural ecosystems, to those which are at a greater and greater remove from them. The prospects, mainly illusory, of moving to 'modern' lifestyles with their attendant affluence, comforts and stylistic gimmicks has seduced whole communities away from their cultural roots. This has resulted in their becoming careless of nature. It has also resulted in their willingness to allow their natural environment to be destroyed or hijacked for 'development', for they see this 'development' ultimately leading them to the promised land.

Another type of condition which has led to the destruction of the environment—apart from the depradations of wars, including civil wars—has been that of abject poverty. Where communities have been reduced to a state of penury, they have been forced to commit ecological suicide in order to survive. For a nation to allow itself to reach a point where its people can only survive by destroying the environment, is to have gone too far.

The Alibi

For many years now the imperative to 'develop' or to 'alleviate poverty' has been used as an alibi for the degradation of the environment.

The Development Imperative: Three Arguments

While attempting to justify large projects like dams, industries or power stations which threaten the environment, it has often been argued that development must not be stopped or hindered. When pressed further, at least three types of arguments seem to have been offered.

The fact that one or more of these three arguments has been used often, and successfully, to justify environmental degradation for the past many years is at least partly due to their seductive logic which feeds into prevailing fashionable positions regarding development (especially within 'developing' countries) and the 'poor'. Hence before examining the three arguments a few cogent points may be made in a preliminary way.

If, in fact, environmental destruction promoted development and helped the poor, then the world would be a much simpler place to live in. On the other hand, if protecting the environment would, by itself, solve the problems of underdevelopment and poverty, then the world would be a much happier place.

International imperatives to invent a term which would permit 'business as usual' in the development sector while accommodating the growing global sensitivity to the environment, led to the coining and popularization of the term 'sustainable development'. Despite its vagueness, for a while it seemed that it might be an effective antidote to the alibis for environmental degradation. However, the alibis continue to be offered without almost any change, and therefore need to be properly assessed. In fact, the earlier reticence over including the environmental dimension in development strategies has been given up since the environmental dimension was translated into the concept of 'sustainable development'. The latter has given rise to programmed ambivalence, as it were, under which developmentalists have procured for themselves a new legitimacy for mainstream development policy while giving to the environmentalists a sense that *their* cause has prevailed. The reality is that nothing much seems to have changed in mainstream development policy. There is no genuine striving towards an alternative perspective on development, no ethical shift that makes sustainable development a reality. 'Sustainability' has been adopted as rhetoric, not as an ethical principle which restructures our relationship with the earth and its creatures in the realm of knowledge and arenas of action.

In the absence of an ethical imperative, environmentalism has been reduced to a technological fix and, as with all technological fixes, solutions are seen to lie once more in the hands of manager-technocrats. Economic growth, propelled by intensive technology and fuelled by an excessive exploitation of nature, was once viewed as a major factor in environmental degradation; it has suddenly been given the central role in solving the environmental crisis. The market economy is given an even more significant role in organizing nature and society. The environmentalist label and the sustainability slogan have become deceptive jargon that is used as convenient cover for conducting business as usual.

Let us consider the three arguments.

The First Argument: It is argued that if development is inhibited then the impact on the environment will be even more drastic than the impact of the project in question.

The underlying assumption of the first type of argument is that the more developed a society, the less pressure it puts on the environment. Conversely, the less developed a society, the more the threat to the environment. One, perhaps the most common, interpretation of Mrs Indira Gandhi's oft quoted statement 'poverty is the greatest polluter', made at the Stockholm conference on environment, is this. But on what evidence is this assumption based?

All indicators seem to suggest that the more developed a society (given the current usage of the term development), the greater the burden on the environment. To take the two most significant indicators, developed societies both consume more resources and generate much more waste than developing societies. (Incidentally, it can be shown that developed societies also exhibit more inequalities and disparities than underdeveloped ones. But of course they are also able to export disparities and through that achieve absolute minima at home and thus prevent social upheavals and strife at home.) What developed societies do manage to do, mainly because of the financial clout they have, is to transfer much of the environmental costs to developing societies. The nature of the environmental impact of developed societies is also somewhat different from those of developing societies. Whereas developing societies mainly degrade their soil and vegetation and pollute water with domestic (mainly organic) waste, developed countries tend to pollute the air, emit chemicals into the water and affect the climate and the ozone layer.

But there is another aspect to which the political and intellectual élite of the Third World gets drawn as part of the very seductiveness of the system that I spoke of above. Perhaps the one factor that has fuelled the 'development versus environment' debate more than any other is the injustice in some countries having such high levels of consumption while others have almost nothing. Whereas this sense of outrage is well justified, the resultant zeal to reach the levels of consumption of developed societies is totally unjustified. If the world is to be saved, this sense of outrage should fuel an urge to cut down waste and opulence, rather than to mimic a lifestyle that promotes them.

Perhaps there needs to be a global consensus on consumption and waste levels which are ethical and acceptable based on the earth's capacity to support. And, just like the two child norm for limiting population growth, there need to be consumption norms for protecting the environment.

The call for curbing consumption by limiting growth has been given so often (and mostly on flimsy grounds) that it has lost its credibility. As already argued above, there are no inherent limits to growth, at least none that have yet been discovered. The plea for curbing consumption can, therefore, be based on one or more of the following facts:

- That whereas there is (yet) no known limit to growth, in order to not exhaust natural resources, consumption and waste must not outstrip regeneration and replenishment.

  Therefore, the first 'limit to growth' is a temporal one where the ability to regenerate and replenish must keep pace with the consumption.

- In many cases the growth and consumption of one society are far greater *and at the cost* of another. In such cases justice demands that the high consuming society curb its consumption in order to allow the deprived society to get its due.

Our world, at present, offers us almost nothing but instances of one or both of these scenarios for justifying a control on consumption.

The Second Argument: It is also argued that an overwhelming percentage of people want the 'fruits' of development, especially things like electricity, cars, televisions, videos and air-conditioners.

Whereas this is true in itself, what is often forgotten is that these and other 'commodities' are 'sold' by the marketing mechanism as if they had nothing else but financial costs. If people were asked to choose between drinking water and television or air to breathe and cars, most would opt for water and air. However, though in effect that is the choice before the world, it is never allowed to be presented as such. Individuals who recognize this are made to feel helpless in a system where their own sacrifices would only inconvenience them without either making their lot, or that of the world, any better.

Besides, the market mechanism works on the assumption that every one desires commodities and prefers them over nature. In some sense this is a self-fulfilling prophecy for, in the process of acting on this assumption, the market mechanisms seek to, and partly succeed in, destroying the diversity of tastes and preferences that were inherent in the society. If this diversity was allowed to survive then who knows how many people might prefer lifestyles which were in harmony with nature.

Apart from market mechanisms, the disparities in society also fuel the adoption of unsustainable cultures. A few adopt such opulent lifestyles that the very opulence ensures that only a very few can afford to adopt them. The remaining many aspire to these lifestyles because they have been demonstrated and held up as exclusive (the urge to be exclusive seemingly being primordial). As societies open up and get greater economic and political 'freedom', the aspirations of the many start being satisfied, leading to the collapse of ecosystems. This happens nationally and globally. For example, countries of the West adopted consumption patterns that could only be sustained as long as they exclusively practiced them (and perhaps not even then, as climate change and ozone depletion seem to have demonstrated). However, with the emergence of independent nation states in Asia and Africa, all aspired to live the lifestyles of the 'exclusive' white man (and woman), and having lost their own cultural linkages, their lifestyles became unsustainable. Working at cross purposes, multinational corporations nevertheless continued to promote these unsustainable lifestyles among the newly independent nations, for profit.

Therefore, the preference that most people show for the 'good things' of life is partly because they are made to believe that there are no trade-offs involved, especially not crucial ones, and partly as a result of the marketing mechanism which first seeks to create a demand for a commodity and then seeks to use this demand to justify its production. The demonstration effect in a stratified society of lifestyles of the rich is also considerable. This is further bolstered by a system of communicating the dominant perspective through the mass media while at the same time curbing information on the vital issues people should really be concerned with.

The Third Argument: A third argument is offered both in justification of large projects and also when forest encroachments, or the opening of forests and other protected areas to grazing and fuelwood collection, has to be justified. This argument seeks to justify the resultant environmental degradation by stating that the alleviation of poverty is more important. It is sought to be argued that environmental concerns are élitist, mainly of the rich, and certainly long term, whereas the need of the hour is to give, to the poor, access to biomass.

There are undoubtedly situations where this argument has validity. But, unfortunately, in most cases it seems to be used to cover up other, preferable, opportunities that could be demanded on behalf of the poor. For example, when extraction of fuelwood from forests is justified, what is not mentioned is the failure of the energy policy where a third of the nation's budget is spent on meeting the energy needs of a small proportion of the population. The remaining are priced out of the race and therefore forced to destroy their own forests. Also, the resources provided for growing firewood as a renewable source of fuel for perhaps half the country's population are less than 0.25 per cent of the budget, while those provided for electricity for the remaining half are about 25 per cent.

Similarly, when encroachments on forest land are justified, what is sought to be covered up is that the landless who are encroaching remain landless and, in some cases, have become landless because of the huge disparities, despite their illegality, in landholdings. These landless continue to seek land because of the increasing capital intensiveness of our industrial sector and the failure to provide them with alternative sources of income. The forest is made to suffer because of failures in land reforms and in rural development.

But does all this solve the problem of poverty? In actual fact it aggravates it, for the degradation and destruction of forests adversely affects the soil and water conditions of the region, thereby creating a new class of impoverished who have either lost everything in floods or droughts, or whose lands can no longer support them. These 'noveau poor' are then again persuaded to encroach upon forests as a part of the ongoing strategy to remove poverty . . . *ad infinitum.*

When floods and droughts ravage the countryside then the government has to divert resources for emergency aid and repair at least some of the damage. This means that there is even less money for the poor, further impoverishing them.

Caring for the Environment

At this point we can move into the broader debate on development and environment in which the first task is to identify still relevant issues. Today, it is no longer necessary to establish that environmentally destructive economic growth can only, at best, be short term; that a neglect of the environment seriously inhibits the potential for socio-economic progress; or that economic growth must be equitable and environmentally regenerating if it is to be seen as development. However, despite broad agreement on these points, the process of protecting and regenerating the environment faces many obstacles in India.

Perhaps the most formidable of obstacles is put up by those who attempt to depict conservation efforts as essentially esoteric, this in turn based on environment being depicted as protection of 'wildlife'. It is being put up as a conflict between the interests of 'tigers and trees' on the one hand, and of tribals and poor rural communities, on the other. Such persons argue that wildlife protection is against the interests of the local people, whose needs must take predominance.

Unfortunately, such arguments not only move governments, but also many 'environmentalists'. However, in such a debate what is often forgotten is that the conflict is not really between wildlife and people, but between one class of people and another. It is not the protection of wildlife that is causing the impoverishment of the people, it is the protection of the interests of a few rich people which is causing this.

When people and their livestock are sought to be kept out of sanctuaries or forests, a hue and cry is raised to allow them in on humanitarian grounds, even though this is illegal. However, in almost all such areas there are huge tracts of agricultural lands owned by rich landlords, in violation of land ceiling laws. But there is no corresponding hue and cry to distribute these surplus lands to the poor, even though that would be legal. Besides, if this land was distributed, the poor would not need to destroy the sanctuaries and forests, and thereby their own future.

Recently, the Madhya Pradesh government ordered the opening up of all sanctuaries for the collection of non-timber forest products, even though this was in violation of the Wildlife (Protection) Act, as amended in 1991. All appeals to withdraw this illegal order seem to have fallen on deaf ears.

The next level of impediments has come from those who believe that all 'development' projects are sacrosanct and that the value of even one watt of electricity or one unit of industrial production far surpasses anything found in nature. Such people usually talk about (pay lip-service to?) the importance of protecting the environment ***but quickly add that it should not be at the cost of development.*** The qualification at the end then becomes the justification for pushing through even the most destructive of 'development' projects.

Apart from forgetting that economic growth which is environmentally destructive is neither sustainable nor developmental, such people also forget that whereas the environmental destruction they wreak will affect mainly the poor, much of the short term benefits of their 'development' projects will go to the rich. This is particularly true of capital-intensive development as we have known it over a long period. And yet, in the new setting of global corporate capitalist development, we are being told that all we need is more capital from abroad and 'opening up' ourselves to make that possible.

The segment of society which supports such a pattern of economic growth is willing to totally sacrifice the environment for the production of energy but unwilling to sacrifice a single air-conditioner for the conservation of energy. Such interests will not raise a finger to protect the health of millions of people from the impact of pollution (for example from the Rajghat power station in Delhi) but will move heaven and earth to protect those among themselves who have been responsible for setting up or allowing the operation of such hazardous plants. They will insist on locating 'development projects' at the most environmentally inappropriate sites because political, procedural and administrative interests need, in their opinion, greater protection than the environment (for example the proposed power stations at Bawana, Kayamkullam and Dholpur).

Then there are those who profess to follow the ideology represented by the oft-quoted statement 'poverty is the greatest polluter'. They immediately reduce any discussion on the environment to a discussion on the population, especially the poor population. To them, the masses of poor people are not only the polluters but also the pollutants. They throw up their hands and announce that nothing can be done to save the environment unless population is controlled. They sit in well-lit, wood-panelled offices, with piles of paper around them, and show you pictures of poor rural women carrying headloads of fuelwood out of forests. Unless this can be stopped, they argue, the forests are doomed. Over mutton curry, you are told that it is the goats which are ruining the forests of India !

Incredibly, they see no connection between their own lifestyles and environmental destruction. They don't recognize that, as far as the environment is concerned, it is not the number of people but the number of consumption units that matter. And, that, a family living in affluence in the city consumes thirty to forty times the resources, and generates many times the waste, that a poor village family does. So, the important issue is not the controlling of the population as such, but the controlling of consumption. The same Americans and Europeans who write heart-rending articles and make moving films about the destruction of rainforests in Brazil, also eat the enormous number of hamburgers that necessitate the conversion of agricultural lands in Brazil into grazing lands, and the consequent destruction of the rainforests.

There is no doubt that the much talked of 'population explosion' should be a matter of deep concern, not because it breeds the poor but because it affects the poor and their access to water, tropical forests and other natural habitats, *largely because of the appropriation of these resources by the rich* that has taken place already.

Finally, perhaps the greatest impediment is put up by the government itself. India has among the most comprehensive environmental policies and laws in the world. However, they are continuously ignored and are violated every day. Some argue that perhaps the reason why such progressive policies and laws were allowed to be formulated is because there was confidence that they would never be enforced.

For one, the task of looking after the environment is left almost totally to the ministries and departments of environment, with all other sectors of the government acting as adversaries. There is almost no internalization of environmental concerns within much of the government.

Second, though there is budgeting of financial resources in the government, there is no budgeting of natural resources. As a result there is a constant demand for natural resources without the ability to properly plan and ensure that they are allocated on the basis of optimality rather than on a first come first serve basis.

Third, in order to protect itself from the consequences of violating its own laws, the government operates in almost total isolation and secrecy. Information that could be even minimally embarrassing for the government is zealously guarded. This essentially makes it impossible for the people and their organizations to play the watch-dog role assigned to them by the government itself; or of even exercising their basic rights as citizens in a democracy. People's participation is, therefore, an element of those same policies which is enunciated but not implemented. Once again, environment becomes an arena of doublespeak—and precisely for the reason that current development policies promote both poverty and environmental degradation. The laws and the commitments of government, both to the movement at home and to the international environment lobby, have become a cover for promoting both—and covering up both!

The Environment - Poverty - Development Syndrome

Based on the alternative perspectives presented above and the observations made earlier in the essay in different contexts, I shall sum up the broad position on the relationship between environment and poverty.

Three sets of relationship have emerged: between environment and development, between development and poverty and between environment and poverty, apart from the one between all three and the political system.

- There is no doubt that the present dominant model of development, all along perceived globally—across cultural specificities and physical and ecological diversities—but increasingly 'globalized', has engendered forces that have both led to gross disparities and other attendant phenomena, all reinforcing existing states of poverty and increased erosion of the environment through phenomena like deforestation, erosion of the soil, pollution and increasing shortages of water and access to land and what are known as common property resources. As was pointed out quite early, the goal of development, following its economistic paradigm, is the creation of wealth rather than elimination of poverty. And the two do not necessarily go together.
- The ongoing debate pitching development against environment seems to be set in a North-South rhetorical context which merely skims over the basic debate on environment and poverty.

There is much reason to argue that on grounds of both the socio-economic—and political—conditions in which the people are placed as well as on those of ecological stability and balance (though not necessarily ecological conservation at every stage) the issue of poverty and its constituent causes ought to receive priority in social policy. As hinted, there may be transient processes which may affect the environment but it is also clear that in the long run perpetuation of poverty can only hurt the ecological base of the social order while efforts to wage a struggle against it—though not through the present development paradigm aimed at accumulation *per se*— must deal also with issues of environmental degradation and degeneration.

There are two other related conceptual points. First, 'poverty' is only a summation of a variety of concrete phenomena—growing disparities both in the living standards of individuals and communities and their regional and ethnic contexts, rising unemployment and underemployment producing marginalization and declining access to vital resources, *social* discrimination producing what we described earlier as 'social poverty' and, of course, ecological deprivation leading to what we termed 'ecological poverty'.

Second, there is the phenomenon of not just poverty at a given time but of accentuation thereof through processes of impoverishment, destitution, etc. This latter is closely related to declining access to natural resources and community assets which too are grounded in natural resources. It is also related to growing vulnerability to disease and insanitary conditions which too are often caused by high rates of environmental pollution, congestion and the like.

Beyond this 'deepening' of the states of poverty lies the whole issue of declining access of the poor to the power structure of society and to sources of influence and decision-making, the whole phenomenon of *disempowerment*. To a large extent this is caused by growing gaps and conflicts of interest engendered by the development process, the poor being put at a greater and greater remove from the locus of planning and governance and, poverty being abstracted away as a statistical category—thus promoting in the people a growing sense of inadequacy and incompetence, and over time inducing in them a sense of marginality. The issue —of poverty and disempowerment—becomes more serious as the economy becomes more internationalized and globally 'integrated' and the excluded people find themselves further removed from information that is vital to their lives and livelihood and their chances of survival. But alongside these typical political dimensions is also the environmental dimension of being torn away from their natural roots—as well as from their community and cultural ties—producing in them an even deeper sense of isolation. Environment is one dimension around which a sense of unity and common purpose exists; it ties people together, including across class and other—caste and religious—barriers.

With the question of power and a sense of empowerment is also tied the whole sense of social purpose, in this case the issues of equity and justice. One of the central problems here is of linking the protection and sustenance of the environment with the protection, sustenance and enhancement of levels of living of the large mass of the people as per the 'rights' obligated by society and the State. In respect of the larger development process, it is an issue of how to restructure development (local, national, global) in ways that simultaneously alleviate poverty and conserve/regenerate/enhance environmental conditions.

More simply put, we can think of *poverty as deprivation*. There can be primordial (or fundamental) deprivation, as when basic nutrition, a sense of security and self-value and a conducive living environment are denied. And there can be acquired deprivation when a certain standard of living or social status is denied. Put in more familiar language, the first thing that can be said about poverty and environment is that certain aspects (elements) of the environment are a part of the 'minimum needs basket', the basket which contains items such that the absence of any one of them would mean impoverishment. The second thing that can be said about poverty and environment is that many other things in the basket are such that their availability (essentially) presupposes a vibrant natural environment.

It would be reasonable to suppose that the following would be an essential part of any 'minimum needs basket':

- Adequate quality of water for drinking and other uses
- Minimal quality of drinking water
- Minimal quality of air
- Uncontaminated and safe food
- Food security
- Physical security (from hazards, disasters)

Apart from these, there are other basic needs which are also dependent on the environment, but not so directly. These are:

- Shelter
- Fuel and energy
- Recreation

Though modern technology has made it possible to meet these needs in a manner which does not necessarily presuppose a high level of ecological balance, in much of the 'developing' world, for much of the population, these needs are still met directly from the environment and,therefore, any degradation of the environment has a direct impact on poverty.

Finally, in a very general sense, the environment is the world of matter, and if that is destroyed, all life will cease.

One way of looking at 'destructive' development is to see it as being characterized by:

- Using natural resources in a way and, at a rate, that exceeds their ability to regenerate.
- Dumping wastes (quantity and type) which cannot be assimilated.
- Creating artificial compounds (or releasing constituent particles) such, and/or in quantities such, that they are hazardous to health and environment.
- Diverting natural resources from subsistence to luxury uses.
- Diverting natural resources from the 'many poor' to the 'few rich'.
- Creating and promoting consumption patterns which demand all the five preceding processes.
- Creating vested interests, within and outside the government, to support such consumption patterns.
- Promoting the development of technologies and processes of consumption and waste at rates much faster than the technologies of regeneration and protection.
- Polarizing societies where one class reaps benefits of ecological destruction while another pays the price.

Environment, Poverty and Human Rights

That brings us to the need to locate the whole issue of poverty and environment in the context of fulfilment of people's rights, within the broad framework of the struggle for human rights.

Once again, corresponding to the dichotomy between development and environment being stressed by developmental planners and politicians is their rhetoric about the primacy of economic over civil and political rights. Both dichotomies are being used to push élitist notions of development, hi-tech industrialization, consumerist standards of consumption and growing State control over natural resources like forestry and timber, rainforests, land, mines and sites where toxic wastes are being dumped by foreign corporations, often with the connivance of local administrators and politicians, as well as on wildlife and various species of plants. These dichotomies are of course being pressed in the name of the 'people' and 'poor people' in particular. The rights of indigenous peoples, tribals and various other communities found to sustain themselves through access to natural resources are being trampled upon in the name of development, national sovereignty and 'the people' of the developing world.

The Malaysian Prime Minister, Dr Mahathir bin Mohamad, is the most ardent and vociferous advocate of such a model of development but there are a great many Third World governments, planners as well as environmentalists, who employ the Mahathir jargon of ending Northern hegemony by the South catching up with the North through full-scale industrialization including the destruction of community forests and land rights and the use of highly repressive methods (including repressive legislation as well as intimidation of environmental and human rights activists) against individuals and movements that are engaged in stopping such destruction. And all this in the cause of integration into the world economy as well as incorporating traditional peoples and their lifestyles into the modern global culture—the latter and those who espouse their cause being branded as 'traitors' who are standing in the way of developing countries' progress.

There are many other violations of human rights (both political and cultural) that are being swung in the cause of 'development' that is being increasingly aimed not for but against the poor and the deprived—restricting access to land including village commons and grazing rights, turning a blind eye to landowner violence against the landless and in fact agents of the State aligning with the former, land alienation on behalf of commercial (including foreign) interests, forcibly moving out urban squatters and 'outsiders' including 'environmental refugees' and, above all, forcing the eviction of entire communities for development projects like large dams and thermal and nuclear plants. The Narmada project represents the most widely discussed and documented among the latter but there are a whole array of such projects which are being promoted in the name of development, and ostensibly in the name of providing energy and water and increased agricultural productivity to backward areas and the 'people', including the 'poor' and the 'backward'!

Conclusion

Based on the various steps of my analysis, I will now draw an overall profile of environment and poverty in the present context of development and the politics thereof. It appears that environment is emerging as the last frontier of both the imperialist drive of world hegemony and 'world order' and the national chauvinist drive of Third World élites posed in anti-Western terminology but in fact falling prey to the globalization of the world economy. In this, unfortunately, leading NGOs including environmental NGOs are joining, considering themselves Third World nationalists and engaging in anti-North rhetoric but in the process providing support to national élites and bureaucrats pursuing development strategies aimed against the poor and diverse local communities, and themselves (the environmentalists) leaving behind the old community contexts of their activities and getting drawn into the politics of globalization.

As already argued earlier, the key parameter of saving or destroying the environment, especially from the point of view of the poor, is to be found in the nature of the political system that addresses itself to this issue. The prevailing political system—both in domestic settings and in the international domain—seems to militate against enlisting the environmental dimension (including its human rights component) on behalf of the poor and the oppressed and the increasingly marginalized and excluded sections of the social order. But it is still conceivable to come forward with an alternative design that at once preserves the environment and empowers the poor. The task of enlisting nature and its vast pool of resources and potentialities—which are still immense—is essentially a political one.

Reorientating Development

This is perhaps a good point to look at the approach to development strategy pursued in India (as well as elsewhere) so far and to arrive at an understanding of what could be the most appropriate approach for a poor country that is riven by deep dissensions and a growing polarization between a small privileged class and large sections of people who are marginalized and excluded from the mainstream development process. In what follows I will be less concerned with specific policies being pursued on which I may agree or disagree than with the broad philosophy of development that I find appropriate for our situation.

Before I do this let me say that the whole conception of 'development' that has emerged in the last half-century represents one of the most powerful of the positivist thrusts that human intelligence has conceived. It involves a massive intervention in the whole social process—and the process of history—as well as an intervention in the institutional matrix of civil society based on a whole new mode of thinking about social goals. Development, if well conceived, can open up vast spaces for struggling humanity but, if misconceived or miscarried, can spell disaster, both for the people and for the social fabric. Hence the need to tread with great care and a sense of responsibility when embarking upon any definitive course of development such as in planning for the whole society.

Development Strategy: Alternative Conceptions

Having said this, let me consider the current approach to development. There are two levels or modes at which the approach has been conceived. The first of these has to do with fulfilling the minimum needs of the people, removing the sources of poverty and marginalization, focusing on pressing problems like unemployment and devising an institutional strategy (e.g., decentralization) through which all this can be achieved. There has, however, been another way that development has been perceived, which happens to be the dominant trend even now. This is the path of going for all the latest technologies, of catching up with industrialized countries, of becoming more competitive in the international market, of integrating with the world economy, of providing the sinews of high capitalism through hi-tech and high-profile industrialization. This is in keeping with the predominant thrust in development literature, especially for large countries, which is to go for big things and aim at becoming a leading industrial and technological power on the world scene. The fact that the latter vision would end up benefiting only a minority, leaving the masses at the mercy of the State and of corporate capital does not seem to discourage its proponents. But can the first approach to focusing attention on pressing tasks at home hold water against world trends? I happen to believe that it can. But for this we need to have clarity and courage on the question of whom one is planning for as well as a willingness to come down from abstract academic formulations to ones that are intelligible to the people at large.

The main issue we face is of the failure of the system to deliver the goods of the basic and minimum kind for all, of providing minimum justice, of eradicating the worst forms of exploitation. It is the simple failure of the system through its bureaucratic-institutional framework, not so much a failure of ideology or that of a structural kind, which comes so easily to us analysts and ideologues—and is quite valid at our level—but does not quite reflect the concerns and anxieties that besiege the common man.

We face a curious dilemma here: in trying to achieve a maximal state of performance (raising living standards for all, achieving a fulsome unity of the country in total non-violence, providing a wholly clean government, solving with some finality major problems) we have lost the capacity to fulfil minimal needs, respond to minimal demands, produce a moderate state of justice and cleanliness in public life, control violence in the social order, bringing it down to tolerable limits. But what the people are asking for is the latter, not the former. They would no doubt welcome the former (viz., a perfect state) if it were possible but that is not what they are asking for.

Irrelevant Utopia

This may sound less ambitious and may not satisfy our proclivity to build perfect utopias but it is in fact more basic. We have never really thought of fulfilling people's democratic aspirations in this manner, namely fulfilment of a package of minimum provisions and facilities for all: In food, in access to drinking water, in health and nutrition through paramedical and ancillary services; through education that focuses on literacy and elementary and vocational education for all; through transport and roads and 'area planning' that are provided through the use of intermediate and relevant technologies; through a system of welfare that caters to absolutely the basic minimum needs of the poor and rural people; through a structure of administration that deals with these minimum demands instead of some more sophisticated and computerized model of governance; through judicial institutions that attend to people's pressing problems and conflicts.

The reason why we have not thought of the economic, social and administrative components of development in any adequate manner is worth going into. The real reason is that we have had for too long, a model of top-down economics that is also intellectually and aesthetically satisfying to the middle class mind, apart from providing to that class a whole structure of privileges and status and lifestyles. We have come up with a model of growth and development that has aimed at prosperity for the nation that is then meant to be shared downwards with the people, rather than by setting modest goals for the people that are automatically shared at the bottom and middle tiers of the economic pyramid and the political structure. Hence, our attachment to centralized planning and decision-making and a hi-tech model of technology that thinks of the people in terms of 'target groups' to which both the planning, technology and development processes and the political and party processes should ostensibly reach.

Top-Down Model

In fact, we have landed ourselves in a rather dangerous situation in which, following a top-down and centralized model of economic development and dispensation of justice, we have created a system that has found itself incapable of dealing with major problems, producing, in the process, a growing discontent and disenchantment among the people and isolation of power centres from them, with a yawning vacuum in the spaces that divide the two. It is in these spaces that deeper pathologies like communalism and 'fundamentalism' find a fertile ground, while the normal democratic process gets stymied and rendered impotent as a result of these maladies.

In the meanwhile, given these growing schisms and yawning gaps, the institutional edifice that we had at one time created has suffered major erosions and a combination of personalized, feudal and 'religious' techno-managerial actors and agents have emerged that have tried to fill the institutional void.

One common characteristic of these three—personalized power brokers, feudal and upper caste alignments using religious bogeys and technocratic and managerial agents—is their attitude to suffering humanity. There is no empathy in their minds for this humanity. For the poor and the powerless, the Dalits, the women and the ecologically impoverished, the tribals and the so-called backward classes. For these, there is no place in the minds of the new élites, some of whom have started operating outside the constitutional framework, lacking in accountability and soon moving into equations and deals that foment a large culture of corruption and influence-peddling. In this culture, not only the whole structure of black money and stashed away funds thrives, but it also leads to trading away our interests as a nation through deals like Bofors and other scandals during the Eighties and through the complete undermining of public trust in major institutions, as happened when the stock market and banking 'scam' broke out on the nation in the early Nineties—an all-out model of the corruption of public life.

The basic message that comes through is fundamental—to think of the democratic yearnings of the people beyond mere electoral battles and into fulfilling basic minima for all instead of some macro framework of prosperity and stability for a few. To move towards a restoration of institutions and, beyond mere restoration, to the creation of new institutions of a decentralized and people-orientated kind. Institutions that can attend to minimum needs and demands and take full cognizance of the suffering and destitution and insecurity and sense of powerlessness of the people.

Emerging Agenda

The agenda that thus emerges is not the spectacular or revolutionary capture of power with a view to producing a national utopia. It is, instead, far more mundane yet far more basic—of taking the people seriously, respecting their thinking and wisdom, producing structures and institutions and technologies that can respond to their needs, and adopting attitudes and values that respond to their voices. Voices from below, voices of the powerless who have so often entrusted power to a political party or a set of parties within the parliamentary framework but whose expectations have all along been belied.

Now this new stirring for change coming from the poor and the oppressed, the Dalits and the tribals, and also from the youth all across the country, more than from the urban middle classes and the intellectuals, is asking from those of us who are committed to making development an instrument of democratic rights something far more fundamental than we have been used to. It harkens us to show our solidarity with the oppressed and the powerless, not in terms of some utopia that we come up with, but in terms of basic and minimum needs that they are concerned about. And similarly rethink our conceptions of national unity, regional and ethnic diversity, and the just and humane demands of the people who have lost confidence in a New Delhi-based conception of the nation state from which they have long felt alienated.

Can we respond to this new striving for socio-economic paths and political and institutional modalities that is inherent in a basic allegiance to the marginalized and excluded people and communities? The scenario we face is in many ways frightening—unless we are willing to have the courage of our convictions to do justice to people and classes and regions whom we have through our own past actions driven out of the system, and to get a sense of power ourselves from a solidarity with those outside the kernel of power.

The fundamental challenge that faces the development community is to not just hold its own against all kinds of detractions and temptations held out by the bureaucracy on the one hand and religious bigots on the other, but to step out of hackneyed structures and take up a completely different agenda that is picked up from the peripheries and built from there.

Vested Interests

Experience suggests that such an agenda will prove unacceptable to vested interests. Thus the approach of the Planning Commission to the Eighth Plan under the National Front government to evolve a social policy (as against a merely economic one) that was aimed at removing inequalities and disparities, exploitation and oppression, and enforcing the rights of the deprived and the excluded and making that the real harbinger of change was successfully resisted by those for whom the new upsurge of consciousness of the restless masses could unleash forces that could upset their already acquired privileges and positions.

As with social policy, so with the cause of the environment. Here, in fact, it is quite clear that the lobby for large hydroelectric and thermal power plants is growing rather than declining. It represents the continuing hold of powerful interests (all the way from local contractors to the World Bank) and a carry-over of the earlier mind-set.

What we have is a great deal of political ferment at the very bottom of society which is sought to be cleverly contained by the bureaucratic machine. There is little doubt that the biggest stumbling block in putting through any programme of change earlier and now is indeed the bureaucracy. Moreover, it is a bureaucracy that has undergone a marked change in its nature and alignments over the past decade. It has become the part of a global nexus of interests, a nexus with the corporate sector and a nexus with corrupt elements in the political structure. It has become increasingly technocratic in nature, with the computer leading the way. And by its enormous spread and consolidation at the top, it has become highly centralized and has ceased to be an 'all India' service.

One should not be surprised at these contradictions and resistances. They are to be expected in any programme of change. The point is to be able to muster up enough political will and undertake necessary institutional restructuring, above all of the administrative machinery. Only then can the contradictions be resolved and resistances overcome, and the vested interests that lie behind them defeated.

In that lies the challenge of change.

Towards an Alternative Package

There has been a lot of thought given to such a 'challenge of change', both at the macro level in terms of an alternative set of policies and at the micro level in terms of new experiments and initiatives by highly experienced individuals who have committed themselves to realize their dreams on the ground. The former includes employment generation based on the 'right to work', redistributive justice based on both restructuring of class relations at local levels and access to vital resources like land, water and common property resources. It replaces the economistic conception of development based on accummulation and investment *per se* by a socio-political approach that emphasizes equity as an engine of growth. It emphasizes people's participation in development based on the 'right to development' which considers it a human right instead of a techno-managerial fix. It calls for the adoption of a more federal and decentralized model of governance in which the people come forward with their own solutions to the problems they face through direct access to political power and through that to economic power as well. It seeks the opening up of channels of communication and knowledge about issues directly affecting the poor through the 'right to information'. And, through all this, it aims at removing the present imbalances between urban and rural areas, between communities and regions and of course between the mass of the poor and the upper and middle classes who have so far succeeded in pre-empting opportunities and resources and excluding the rest from both the arena of the State and the arena of 'development'. This situation has got further accentuated in the current flourish for integration into the world economy.

Fortunately, this last effort of the Indian élite being bailed out by global and 'globalizing' interests has led to a considerable build-up of opinion against it and this in turn—and this is crucial for us from the point of view of the poor—has once again generated interest in questioning the whole model of development that we had adopted and which was then hijacked by the high consumption élite—landing us in a debt trap and a serious BoP crisis—and in the need to move towards an alternative strategy of development.

Micro Initiatives

This may be a good point at which to draw upon some of the more interesting efforts at 'alternative development' that have been tried out in diverse social and regional settings and in which different kinds of actors—from activists to bureaucrats to struggling masses—have been involved.

There are of course a whole series of highly innovative 'experiments'. There are the widely documented ecological break-throughs achieved in the Chipko movement, both through the larger efforts of Sunderlal Bahuguna and others at inspiring people to engage in building a new kind of community that is at once conducive to nature and struggling against all kinds of vices and detractions (from drinking to marketization) and through the patient and persistent efforts of people like V.D. Saklani to resuscitate nature from a state of total erosion to its full glory. There is the equally widely acclaimed model village of Ralegaon Sindi in the Parner tehsil of Ahmednagar under the inspiring leadership of Annasaheb Hazare, giving us a truly self-reliant, socially non-exploitative, environmentally non-toxic and politically resilient community.

There are many other experiments providing us with atypical and 'out of this world' efforts. But there are also a whole series of efforts by simple folk. A Harijan teacher, in Rasmal Nasirpur near Mathura, rising from a sub-human background of filth, deprivation and social ostracism, by the sheer dint of his perseverence, rising to not just overcome both social and official attitudes but building a 'model school' where Thakurs, Brahmins and Banias vie to send their children to his school. A simple social service organization, in impoverished Vypeen island (close to Kochi in Kerala), by just spreading information on a variety of government schemes meant to help poverty-stricken slum dwellers, at once stopping the exodus from the village and opening up employment and income generating opportunities in the village, ultimately helped lead to a 'come back to the village' movement. A traditional village community in Nagaland launching a modern equivalent called the Common Fund Programme of an ancient practice under which the village assembly was the custodian of common belongings of the village, both rejecting the industrialistic ethic of modernity and replacing government planning by people's participation, in the process answered the key question: poverty is to be eradicated but is there enough fellow feeling for the poor, or if people's participation is the new slogan, should not the poor themselves insist on removing poverty?

Then there are a whole series of small and localized efforts that question macro thinking. A movement of committed Gandhians located in Gujarat stridently working towards delegitimizing the excesses of modern technology, especially nuclear technology, through a cycle yatra. An equally strident movement on behalf of the tribals not just opposing wrong developmental decisions like the setting up of a steel plant in the private sector with foreign collaboration that threatened to forcibly displace and evict entire communities as happened in Mavalibhata in the Bastar district of Madhya Pradesh, but also calling into question the whole model of development that has engendered such decisions. The efforts of a 'people's Collector' in the Nilgiris district who, given the mandate of solving the problem of preventing alienation of tribal land and convinced of the rights of the tribals under the Indian Constitution, went about his task so methodically and with such vigour that all efforts to transfer him led to massive indictment from various quarters and when he was finally transferred under the pressure of vested interests, led to a virtual 'people's movement' against such action. Or the atypical undertaking by a Professor (and that too from the Indian Institute of Management, Ahmedabad) to document various people's initiatives in mobilizing traditional knowledge ranging from organic farming and pesticides to engineering and industry through *Honey Bee* (a journal brought out in six languages) that not only documents and disseminates innovations produced by farmers and artisans but also lobbies 'for protecting the intellectual property rights of grassroot innovators'. These efforts are varied, continuous, together providing a countervailing culture of development against the dominant one.

What is presented here is no more than a limited cross-section of 'people's initiatives', the 'people' including both the poor and the dispossessed and the sensitive and highly movitated individuals placed in positions of power and influence who however refuse to be part of the exploitative structure of 'development' and of the 'State'.

Towards an Alternative Policy Frame

There are many people who feel that impressive as the various micro experiments are, and exemplary as the individual initiatives on behalf of the poor and the oppressed are, these are still fragmented and often isolated efforts and unless there is scope for either replicating individual efforts on a wider scale or persuading the 'system' to adopt the perspectives underlying them, there is not much hope for transforming the social reality in any significant way. There is much force in this observation but for two points. First, that had it not been for these diverse 'grassroots' interventions—which incidentally are spreading and involving literally thousands of 'activists'—the situation facing the mass of the people, given the growing exploitation and repression of the larger system, would have been far too serious to contemplate or withstand. Second, to the extent that these initiatives work, open up spaces and create hope, they make it possible for those committed to an alternative model of development to keep struggling against the 'system'. And yet, having made these points, there is little doubt that one should keep working towards laying out the broad framework of an alternative perspective. In what follows, I have provided a modest statement of such a perspective in the form of a set of policy parameters, again not in the form of some grand utopian model as in terms of a set of principles and foci of a development effort meant to fulfil basic needs and respond to minimal demands of the people.

Focus on Man

The prime concern of economic policy for a just social order ought to be to generate employment that is at least able to absorb the new additions to the adult population. And, where there is a substantial backlog of unemployment and underemployment, to absorb as large a segment of that as is possible to do by a sheer shifting of the focus of development to employment instead of growth *per se*. The major source of injustice today is to be found not so much in a condition of general scarcity as in the fact of diminishing marginal utility of man as such, in the fact that hundreds of millions of people throughout the world find themselves idle and useless, often in the very prime of their youth.

Agricultural Transformation

The major impetus for such employment will have to come from a transformation of the agricultural sector, converting it from an area of stagnation to a catalyst for growth. While the new technology associated with the Green Revolution may have provided a major breakthrough for nations wanting to achieve self- sufficiency as well as for raising the status of agriculture in national priorities, there is need to adopt these practices with conscious care and to adapt them to fulfil social goals. They must substantially raise employment and the incomes of the poor, not just aggregate output. Beyond availing of the new inputs there is need to attend to other practices: crop differentiation that can increase the amount of labour needed per acre of land and raise the income of labourers, development of water resources that are suited to the needs of small farmers and tenants, encouragement of farm practices that are labour-intensive, discouragement of mechanization that is labour-replacing and the provision of relevant credit and infrastructural inputs for the small cultivators. This, in turn, calls for the other package of measures known as land reforms, so that the benefits of the Green Revolution are widely dispersed instead of being pre-empted by the well-to-do farmers as has occurred so far, so that the rural social and economic structure becomes more egalitarian, and so that the available land is able to provide employment and a minimum income to millions more than is presently the case.

Rural Industrialization

In large parts of the world it is safe to predict that the sum total of reforms involved in the new agricultural technology and redistributive legislation will not be enough to sustain a growing population on land. Studies from several countries on manpower absorption by different sectors of an economy show conclusively that, except in places with very low density and large surpluses of land, there comes a stage when agriculture begins to absorb a diminishing proportion of the rising population. It does not follow from this, however, that those not engaged in agriculture should take to the cities for jobs in modern industries, for the fact is that the latter are better employers of machines than of human beings. And, in any case, the investment needed to generate the needed employment through modern industry is of a scale that few among the poorer countries can afford—except by large-scale import of foreign capital, which entails serious costs from the point of view of both equity and self-reliance.

The usual haphazard growth of towns and cities that takes place in the absence of conscious policy results in their getting trapped into what are essentially parasitic spots where middlemen bring the flashy output of industries from large cities (which cannot be realized any more) and tempt villagers into buying them at exorbitant prices. This should give place to a conscious policy of decentralized industrial development and location so that urban growth becomes complementary to rural development and contributes further to the growth of employment and incomes of the poorer strata. The encouragement of self-employed artisans, the cultivation of the finer arts and crafts according to different national traditions, and the growth of new and small-scale industries for the manufacture of goods needed by the local people can provide the basis for such regeneration.

Social Continuum

The crux of such a combination of policies designed to raise employment and alleviate mass poverty is to put agricultural and rural development at the core of public policy. But there is a counterpart to this approach in the area of urban development and industrial policy as well. Apart from heavy industries that require large capital inputs and centralized organization, industrial development should be employment-oriented as much as possible, should produce goods that are needed by a large strata of the population rather than by a small middle class, and should be widely dispersed so that the employment that it generates benefits all areas rather than being concentrated in a few cities or regions as is the case today. Regional disparities constitute a crucial dimension of social injustice and its visibility. Most of the favoured regions are those with large urban centres.

Socially, this means that the present duality of city and countryside must give place to a continuum in which the Green Revolution (and its necessary concomitants in livestock and horticultural development) regenerates the villages, small-scale and medium industries are located in the towns, and large-scale industries that necessitate heavy inputs of capital and high technical efficiency are located in the cities. As such a fusion between industry and agriculture takes place, further intermediate links in this continuum—rural social structures in towns, urban amenities in villages—can develop, thus combining the potentialities of both rural and urban life and producing a composite and integrated culture.

So conceived, the emerging social reality will not be one made of millions of self-contained villages (as was Gandhi's dream which cannot be realized any more) but, rather, one of thousands of small nucleating towns towards which the rural landscape gravitates, thus doing away with both the present duality of metropolitan and rural cultures, limiting the large size and concentrated location to just the industries that cannot do without them, while at the same time enlarging the size and horizon of rural communities, and providing them with the necessary infrastructure of welfare and communication facilities. Such a spatial continuum—supported by a decentralized structure of community decision-making as argued below—would provide the necessary framework for the techno-economic alternative to the present dualist model of city versus countryside.

Policy on Education

It is not simply by altering the economic basis of rural-urban relationships that a more just social order can be created. We also need to alter the cultural underpinnings of the present patterns of dominance and disparity. An important aspect of the sharp duality of lifestyles and living standards is the nature of the educational system whose aim continues to be to produce colonial-type gentlemen, disorientated from the larger society and constituting a class apart. Meanwhile, a majority of the population continues to be illiterate and unskilled. Studies in this area suggest that expansion of literacy and primary education produce very rich and rapid dividends; acquisition of a minimum educational level greatly raises a person's skills and his capacity to enter the employment market; it also raises his sense of potency and his ability to relate himself to the outside world, his sense of political efficacy, and his general self-confidence and sense of dignity. As I have argued earlier in this essay, crucial to empowering the poor in their struggles against exploitation are access to basic education, health, housing and other social prerequisites. This is central to the need to think of poverty as a social phenomenon and of coming forward with a social policy to deal with it.

There is need to give special attention to the education of women. In most parts of the developing world, women are less educated than men, in countries with low literacy levels women are far less literate than men, and within the depressed social strata and ethnic minorities in these countries, the gap is even more pronounced. These gaps in education among women and between them and men are an important source of the persisting duality of cultures, economic levels and consumption standards. The latter more often than not is a direct function of the perennial shopping to which the educated women are so addicted. These differences also account for the wide divergences in the way children of the rich and the poor are brought up, thus perpetuating sharp disparities for decades to come. A greater attention to raising the educational levels of women and mothers from the poor, underprivileged and conservative strata of society can spin off a major process of social reconstruction.

Ethic of Consumption

As serious as the gaps in the literary culture are the gaps in the material culture that divide the urbanized upper and middle classes from the people. Perhaps the most important and glaring contrast in a poor country is caused by the extraordinary consumption levels and material possessions of the richer and high-status groups, following almost *in toto* the standards set by the high-consumption societies. The lust for things and for more and more things has become so myopic that it has given rise to all kinds of unethical practices, chief among these being a large incidence of corruption among public officials and a thriving black money economy that is sustained by the availability of a large array of luxury consumer goods.

Apart from the vulgarity of such ostentatious living in societies characterized by massive poverty and malnutrition and apart from the creeping corruption to which it gives rise, such standards of consumption also undermine the whole fabric of economic policy. If a massive programme of employment and social welfare is to be generated, a high rate of savings and capital accumulation will be necessary. This implies a large dose of taxation of the rich as well as a high rate of savings among those with large incomes. But it also implies a restraint on salary and wage increases among the employed classes, including the working class, so that resources can be transferred to employing the unemployed (in a poor country to be employed is itself a privilege) and raising income levels of the poorly employed and the underemployed.

All of this calls for an ethic of consumption that discourages ostentatious living, cuts down the production and consumption of non-essential items, and shifts production priorities towards fulfilling the needs of the poor. It is, of course, necessary to encourage saving among the peasantry, the lower-middle classes and even the labouring classes as mentioned above. But this will be an impossible task unless the pace-setters of society themselves adopt a consumption ethic that encourages austerity and reduces the gap in material culture between the different classes. Gandhi put his finger on the most crucial dimension of moving towards a just social order when he called for a limitation of wants and warned his countrymen against falling prey to an industrial machine that not only reduces the majority of men into labouring slaves but also dictates what and how men should eat, wear, dress, sing and dance. Today his insights are even more relevant than they were when he was alive. If there is to be peace and harmony in the world and an end to exploitation among men and nations, the present norm of a high-consumption ethic must give place to one that on the one hand meets the minimum needs of all men and women and on the other limits the needless expansion of wants that have no relationship with the basic requirements of body and mind.

Nature of Production

Built into such an ethic of consumption is also an ethic of production that is critical to the achievement of justice in society. Part of the problem is that both production and distribution are thought of in terms in which the mass of the people are reduced to a position of subjects and onlookers. An economic ethic that seeks to meet the consumption needs of all while limiting the flow of inessential commodities involves a simultaneous increase in the incomes of the poor and the output of goods that they will need to buy with those incomes. This means that instead of conceiving production and consumption as two separate activities, one aims at an economic system that (to repeat Gandhi's dictum) not only produces for the mass of the people but one in which the mass of the people are also the producers.

As are all visions, perhaps this, too, is an ideal type. All that one can hope to initiate is a movement toward such a state. In practical terms this calls for a location policy that, while permitting large-scale organization where it is unavoidable, will encourage the growth of small-scale, labour-intensive, decentralized patterns of industrial development. Similarly, the market economist's retrogressive concept of effective demand (that only the needs that are backed by the existing distribution of purchasing power are worth producing for) will have to give place to a concept of need effectiveness so that the real needs of the people as a whole determine what goes into the package of production. A combination of such a production system and the consumption ethic outlined above will lead to a climate in which progress toward dispersal and decentralization of economic power becomes possible. As this happens, the orientation to social justice will become less technocratic and become more political and thus capable of initiatives from below.

Health and Other Social Minima

A major casualty of the present structure of consumption and production is the fact that large numbers of people suffer from acute malnutrition and resulting physical and mental deficiencies. Their numbers are likely to increase in the next few decades. While national and international bureaucrats are busy propagating birth-control measures to ward off an 'explosion' sometime in the next century, the problem of enabling those who are already born and will be born in the next twenty-five to fifty years to live a normal life and put in sustained work for their livelihood is receiving inadequate attention. The picture of the poor that emerges from various studies is highly depressing: it is a picture of large families exhibiting physical and psychic abnormality, an incapacity for sustained work even for a few hours, a pronounced inferiority complex, a tendency to deal with patterns of exploitation and coercion by directing them inward and against their own dependents, and a vicious cycle of parents inducting children into these characteristics of deprivation and degradation, turning them into the same kind of adults when they grow up, and thus almost *ad infinitum.* We must give top priority to a programme of providing basic health care and an adequate supply of protein and other nutrients to the poor and especially to their children. It is only after a minimum standard of health is assured—and the benefits of education are widely spread—that people's perception of the survival of infants and family size will change and the problem of population growth will be tackled on a rational basis. Alongside minimum levels of income there is need for certain essential *social* minima (varying, of course, according to diverse cultural and climatic conditions) that should be provided for all.

Political Economy of Justice

I have deliberately gone to some length in outlining the precise policy perspectives and corresponding ethics of behaviour needed for the realization of justice in a world marked by extremes of disparity and iniquity. It is only on the basis of such detailed considerations that a more general perspective on goals and strategies for the future can be concretely stated. I shall do the latter now.

Development for Justice

As is already implied in the position I took in the chapter on environment and poverty, I reject the notion that nations of the Third World ought to follow policies that will bring them to the same level as the industrially advanced nations. Such an aspiration is undesirable. It is undesirable because bridging the gap with the rich nations in a short span of time entails exclusive concentration on growth rates and a neglect of the progress toward social justice. And yet it is only the latter that constitutes development. It is necessary to make a distinction between growth and development. By itself, to aim at a high rate of growth of the Gross National Product is unexceptionable; indeed, a noticeable increase in the employment and incomes of the poor is not possible without a significant increase in GNPs. But it is equally true that one can have a fairly high rate of growth of GNP without increasing employment and the income of the mass of the people. In other words, whereas social justice *entails* a high rate of growth of GNP, such growth does not *ensure* justice. And, from the experience we have had so far, it could well mitigate against a just social order.

Minima and Maxima

The analysis so far leads me to the elements of an alternative model. The objective of development, according to me, should be to achieve minimum conditions of material welfare for all the people, the minima to be defined according to local conditions and norms, some societies fixing them higher than others but all of them providing at least a package of minimum items of human necessity such as food, clothing, shelter, nutritional needs of children and mothers, and socially approved minima of health, education, drinking water and public transportation for all.

A policy of minima entails a policy of maxima. Indeed, without the latter the former is, in practice, impossible to realize in reasonable time. Also, beyond a certain point, incomes ought not to be allowed to grow nor human wants allowed to be artificially stimulated by the aggressive salesmanship of modern industry or the demonstration effects from the rich capitalist countries. There are two reasons for this limitation, one of which is relative and the other absolute. No one has a right to amass more and more income and riches when large sections of the population live below subsistence standards. Also, it is morally undesirable to go beyond a certain level of fulfilment of human needs. For, an unlimited gratification of wants leads to individual decay and social disharmony, an unnecessary destruction of natural resources, a fouling up of the human environment, and hence a bartering away of the health and happiness of future generations for the present pleasure and lust of a few. Hence Gandhi's emphasis on the 'limitation of wants'.

There should be a reasonable scale connecting the minima and maxima. That is to say, an admissible ratio between the two, thus limiting disparities and enabling society to implement the principles of natural justice. Entailed in the norm of such a scale is the further norm of transfer of surplus incomes and wealth from those above the maximum to those who have not yet reached the minimum.

Together, the notions of minima and maxima, a reasonable scale between the two, and transfers from the rich to the poor provide us with an economic philosophy not just for a particular country but for the world as a whole. For, it also suggests that countries that have already achieved prescribed levels of material well-being have no right to bottle up resources in the name of national sovereignty and self-aggrandizement. On the other hand, I have no intention of suggesting that international transfers of resources and wealth should take the form of 'aid' from the rich to the poor countries as we understand the term at present, for it is clear that aid policies have seriously compromised the autonomy and self-respect of recipient countries and of individuals living in them. Such autonomy is an integral part of my conception of justice. In fact, I am not interested in bridging the gap between rich and poor countries as an end in itself but, rather, am interested in seeing that the acquisitive spirit that has taken hold of the richer countries does not remain a vehicle of injustice and destruction on a world scale as is the case at present.

Issue of Participation

Implicit in the preferred model for social and economic justice are also a number of other issues. The norms of minima and maxima are not mere economic formulations; they are part of a certain conception of a good and desirable life. Not only should an individual be entitled to a minimum level of living; he should also be able to participate actively (though he ought not to be forced to do so) in the way things are produced and decisions are made. It is not just a minimum wage that one thinks of here in some kind of a contractual relationship, alienated from the work process and the total scheme of ownership, production, and distribution of the means of livelihood. Rather, one thinks of an apparatus that man himself controls, finds meaningful, and derives a sense of personal power and significance from. Furthermore, to the extent that economic activity is managed and mediated by political and administrative agencies, the whole problem of effective participation in decision-making, at the desirable level and in optimum units, becomes real. Without such participation the economic aims may indeed be difficult to achieve.

There is also the question of not permitting the economic process, and what is tellingly called the 'industrial-bureaucratic complex' of modern society, to take on an automation of its own and destroy every other value in its inexorable march. In other words, as the values of a participatory democracy and of non-violence in man's relations to man and to the environment are joined with the values of autonomy and justice, it may well be that we should ask ourselves equally basic questions about the kind of institutional superstructure that we want to build. Three major dimensions of this issue are:

- The rural-urban structure of the economy;
- The territorial structure of the State; and
- The participatory structure of the polity.

As we pose these questions, it will become clear that the available model of modernization is not conducive to our goals; that the norm of a necessary shift from a predominantly rural to a predominatly urban structure based on large-scale industrialization may not be the best thing that human intelligence has devised; and that urban metropolitan life, far from being a 'civilizing' instrument, may turn into a structure of manipulation, exploitation and destruction of the very properties of man's natural environment that are essential to human survival.

Similarly, we may also question the norms of centralized government, large-sized states, and big bureaucracies as necessary instruments of national integration and political accountability. And as we question these, we may begin to answer with greater clarity the questions that have so often been raised about local autonomy, about decentralization of functions, powers, resources, and talents and about optimum size for genuine participation of the people.

Our model of a participatory system should not be conceived in terms of simple political reforms. Rather, it needs to be addressed to a number of sectors—concerning economic organization and its governance, the nature of education, location of work and enterprise, choice of technology, size of units (economic, political, demographic, communications) and the nature of work. Participation is not some process of involving everyone and reducing all to a common denominator. Rather, it consists in evolving institutional structures from which diverse individuals get a sense of dignity and self-respect, as beings that are able to determine their own destinies. Poverty and inequality are themselves reflections not just of prevailing relations of production but rather of structures and values that deny dignity to the human being.

It would be folly, however, to look upon such a perspective as in any way smooth sailing. Nothing is more difficult to realize than changes in the social framework of politics—except for the worse. Every step on such a path needs to be fought for, by organizing for it and building sustained pressures from below in the form of social and intellectual movements. And it is, of course, clear that these will need to be conceived and carried out in not one but many spheres, at not one but many thresholds, and in not one but a large number of societies.

These, then, are the issues that arise when specific problems of economic strategy, political structure, educational policy and the reconstruction of human space are considered from the integrated perspective provided by a political economy of social justice based on the fulfilment of basic needs. As we do this, the distinctions between economic and political issues disappear and new foci of attention gain importance—from the contours of class and culture to ecological considerations to social policy to ethical imperatives. Some of these have already been dealt with in earlier chapters. It is to the remaining that I shall now turn.

Social Policy

In earlier parts of this essay I have had occasion to refer to the need to evolve a social policy as distinct from economic policy both with respect to dealing with the specifically social dimensions of poverty (my argument being that there is a distinct phenomenon of social poverty which cannot be dealt with by economic measures alone and which reveals far deeper levels of human suffering) and in respect of ways of empowering the poor *socially* through inputs that are more varied than mere economic ones. In what follows, however, I will provide a more comprehensive treatment of social policy, providing both a diagnosis of the current situation and a set of policy prescriptions for dealing with it.

Despite more than forty years of democracy and development, India has not been able to resolve the major contradictions inherent in its society. Though this period has seen substantial economic growth, the benefits of this growth have not significantly touched the poorest and most needy sections of society, and have not brought about the social transformation that was anticipated.

This economic growth, apart from being inequitable, has not resolved the various social issues, some historical and others of recent origin, that plague Indian society. Individuals and communities continue to be oppressed because of their ethnicity, geographical location, religion, race, caste or sex. Since the sharp decline in sensitivity of the system to people's grievances, violence is increasingly becoming the universal language of protest and dissent, brutalizing individuals and communities. Social, political and professional institutions are being eroded, and many benign social differences are progressively becoming antagonistic. The lifestyle pursued by the economically better-off strata has proved to be economically and ecologically unsustainable, and is threatening the very basis of survival. Corruption in government and public life is increasing and the State continues to encroach upon the rights of individuals and communities. Subjectively, the poor feel alienated, rejected and excluded from the social structure. This produces in them a sense of inferiority that has become part of social and cultural poverty as distinct from merely economic poverty.

The persistence of these social and economic contradictions is a failure of planning. It is a failure to set in motion social and political processes that alone could have channelized the creative energies of a nation, emerging from centuries of colonialism, towards a path of genuine development.

The Experience Since Independence

In the first fifteen or twenty years after independence, the vision of spreading the benefits of development, providing a regime of economic security and self-reliance for all, and of creating a just social system, energized the nation. The country moved towards self-sufficiency in foodgrains production and in a large array of consumer goods and built up its infrastructure and industrial base. But then the dream began to turn sour. The efforts at enhancing production and productivity were showing results but the socio-political measures required to ensure wide and on the whole equitable distribution of the benefits lagged far behind. The State played a major role in achieving self-reliance for the nation but not for its people, having failed to use its leverage for redistributive measures. The country may have achieved self-sufficiency in food production, and even started producing surpluses, yet large sections of society suffered from malnutrition arising out of a lack of adequate food intake. Indian industry grew at a rapid rate, but so did unemployment, especially as industrial technology became increasingly capital-intensive and labour-displacing. The number of hospitals and schools increased, but sickness and illiteracy remained. Various social amenities became available, progressive laws were enacted, benign policies were formulated, yet access to these declined, there developed a sharp sense of deprivation, social tensions got intensified and society progressively became more turbulent and violent.

By the early Eighties, there was a general sense of despair among many about the process of social transformation. The late Sixties and Seventies had seen an unprecendented rise in social conflicts and tensions and political turmoil. Rejection of efforts to 'discipline the nation' through the authoritarian regime imposed during the national emergency, followed by the failure of the alternate, liberal government to effectively address the main social issues, presented the nation with seemingly few alternatives. Yet another opportunity came in 1989, in the wake of the nation-wide reaction against the rabid corruption and vulgar self-indulgence of the ruling élite. The change in government that took place then set in motion yet another effort at resuming the course of social transformation. It drew upon an array of highly committed individuals. Together they struggled to emerge from an era where the strength of a democracy came to be measured by its ability to suppress dissent. They attempted to reverse the process whereby the path of development allowed only one view of how things must be done for all times, in all places. They affirmed the need to adopt and encourage alternative paths, and pinned their hope on the people, on a model of decentralized governance, on an economic strategy that gave more importance to generating employment and the purchasing power of the people than aggregate growth rates. This proved to be an uphill task, given the continuing power of a colonial state and its bureaucratic stranglehold. Even if that government had lasted, it is not clear that it too would not have failed, like its predecessor in 1977-1979, to provide a real alternative.

During this whole period political thinkers and intellectuals were by and large found to be silent onlookers. The few who spoke out were slow in making themselves heard, while politicians and administrators either continued with a further application of the same old remedies despite knowing that they would not work, or resorted to even more regressive methods in dealing with problems.

The hopelessness of the decade of the Eighties (globally designated as the 'lost decade') polarized perceptions. There were those who blamed everything on the rapidly expanding population, as if that was a cause rather than a symptom of the *malaise* that affected society. There were others who totally capitulated to the 'growth fiends' and put their faith in technological fixes and the vision of 'catching up' with the 'developed' nations. Some even admitted that in taking India to the twenty-first century, many would have to be sacrificed, but that such a price was worth paying. At the same time the middle classes got bewitched into producing more and more for élite consumer standards and this resulted in a self-indulgence and profligacy that sharply polarized the society internally and led to growing indebtedness and dependence externally, rapidly running down foreign exchange resources and pushing the country towards a grave BoP crisis, in the event forcing the government to go in for large scale borrowings, opening up the economy to multinational investors and, for gaining access to these, accepting humiliating conditions imposed by the International Monetary Fund (IMF) and the World Bank. It is thus that we entered the Nineties with fifteen years of turmoil, of failed and abandoned experiments, with a people who were getting more cynical and impatient given the fact that various alternative governments had failed to renew their sense of hope.

Social Policy

It is against this background that we need to conceptualize the whole approach to *social* policy. Conventionally, social policy has been seen as 'non-economic' policy, dealing with 'soft' areas like social welfare, health, shelter, education, culture, etc. Social policy has, therefore, been accorded only residual attention and resources, after the demands of economic policy, which is the preoccupation of most governments, have been satisfied. The need today is for a social policy which cuts across sectors and levels in the government and encompasses all aspects, economic and non-economic, of governance. The need is for a social policy which clearly posits, before the nation, the *social* objectives which must guide all governmental action and must take predominance over merely sectoral interests.

Such a social policy must not restrict itself to a statement of values, for these are changing with time and context. A policy which seeks to postulate universal values, apart from the basic ones like justice, equity and humanity, tends to homogenize and thereby ignore the rich cultural diversities of all nations, especially of one like India. Therefore, social policy must seek to identify appropriate social values and strategies for *diverse* situations. Further, such processes must be institutionalized so that diverse social perceptions and situations can, on a continuing basis, be adequately reflected in the changes that take place in both social and economic strategies.

A social policy must necessarily humanize governance, and be guided by concern for communities and individuals, however small and weak. It must be based on an understanding of past and present social reality, and must seek to build upon historical forces, diverting them from violence and destruction and channelizing them into constructive social processes. In doing this, it must respect the diverse histories and situations of various geographical areas and communities in the country. It must seek to strengthen this diversity, and thereby strengthen the unity, rather than to universalize, homogenize, and thereby weaken.

It follows that the first prescription of a social policy for India must be to *minimize the social and economic oppression* which is currently a part of our social structure. All policies and plans must be measured against this yardstick, and those alternatives which contribute the most to a reduction of inequities must be invariably preferred. Closely related to this first prescription is the need to *defuse social tension and violence* and to *arrest ecological degradation.* These three emerge as the planning priorities for India today.

Reducing Social and Economic Oppression

We live in a society where communities, groups and individuals are oppressed and discriminated against because of their caste, religion, race, sex or age. Though much of this is a historical legacy, consumerism, ecological degradation and inappropriate industrialization and urbanization have added new dimensions to the historical patterns of oppression. Women are tortured and burnt to death for bringing insufficient dowry, children are forced to work eighteen hours a day in factories and mines, in a work environment which is disastrous for their health, or gassed in their sleep because of industrial disasters. Tribals and other rural communities are uprooted from their traditional homes to accommodate development projects and urban and industrial requirements. A majority of village women spend most of their waking life gathering fuel, fodder and water, while their sisters in urban areas increasingly bear the brunt of sexist oppression and molestation.

Indian society is being polarized through injustice. The divide is growing between the oppressor and the oppressed. There is, increasingly, an antagonistic divide between the rich and the poor, the urban and the rural, the male and the female, the adult and the child, the non-tribal and the tribal, the upper castes and the Dalits, the educated and the illiterate, the employer and the employee, the majority and the minority, and the government and the people.

India's Great Poverty

Among the most painful manifestations of social injustice in India is the abject poverty of a large number of its people. A significant proportion of our citizens do not get enough to eat, do not have a secure roof over their heads or enough clothes to cover their bodies with. They have no access to potable water, to education, to economic security or even to an assured prospect of survival. Men, women and children (from the day they can walk) toil from morning to night. Their self-respect, their dignity, their rights—all become subservient to the predominant need for survival. These millions are living out a legacy of misery and malnutrition, a lifetime of semi-starved stupor.

But this great Indian poverty is not a poverty among shortages, it is a poverty among plenty. While millions of children go to sleep hungry every day, the markets are full of luxury and junk food. While millions of people have no roof over their heads, there is enough cement and building material to make thousands of five-star hotels and high-rise luxury flats. While millions of women do not have enough clothes to cover their bodies, India has among the fastest growing textile industries, with the latest in synthetic 'suiting and shirting' overflowing the urban markets. While millions of girls fritter away their childhood, and womanhood, walking longer and longer distances to gather fuel for the hearth, air-conditioners run non-stop in much of urban India, and the latest models of car join the older ones in an endless guzzle of petrol.

India's great poverty is, therefore, not a poverty of resources. It is a poverty of justice.

The Phenomenon of the Two Indias

Underlying these multiple splits in society, there is a fundamental split: a divide between the oppressor and the oppressed, which I have in many of my writings described as the phenomenon of the two Indias.

There is one India which is rapidly progressing towards the twenty-first century, with access to technology, information and resources. This India is comprised of the urban and rural élite, the big farmers, the industrialists, the bureaucrats, the executives and professionals, and the intelligentsia. Though a small percentage of the population, they consume a large bulk of its resources and own, control and allocate the remaining according to their own priorities and interests.

Then there are those who belong to the other India, impoverished, malnutritioned, toiling day and night for survival. They populate much of the country and are an overwhelming majority, 'serving' the first India through daily toil and drudgery (as do the slum-dwellers in the cities and the landless in the villages), but have little say in the manner in which their country, their resources and even their lives are governed. They have little access to technology, information or resources, and are rarely consulted, or even informed, about matters that affect their well-being and survival.

From the perspective of élite India, the sacrifices of these inhabitants of poor India are presumed to be in the 'national interest', their demands for justice are often dubbed as being 'anti-national', their views on matters that concern them viewed as 'unscientific and based on ignorance', and their very existence seen as an acute embarrassment.

Government Initiatives

Poverty alleviation and 'Garibi Hatao' have been government slogans for a long time. Whatever be the economic ideology in fashion, employment generation has always been the key to poverty alleviation, with industry and agriculture being the predominant sources of employment. The government's efforts to blur the divide between the two Indias has broadly been:

- Through legislative and policy measures;
- Through reservations for the weaker sections of society;
- Through direct fiscal measures.

In the last forty years or so, a large number of *laws* have been enacted and *policies* framed, to protect the interests and rights of minorities and the weaker and poorer sections of society. Some of these, like those protecting the personal laws of religious communities or making tribal lands inalienable, are aimed at maintaining the status quo. Others, like those related to land reforms, child labour, minimum marriageable age, etc. are designed to change historical processes of oppression and injustice.

Reservations for members of the minorities and weaker sections of society have been ensured in Parliament, the government, educational institutions and panchayats.

Various *fiscal measures* have also been taken to economically strengthen the minorities and weaker sections of society. Apart from special dispensations to tribal states, and through schemes and programmes for the minorities and economically weaker segments of society, financial concessions have also been given, for example by exempting tribals from income tax. Quotas have been set up to protect the interests of the poor, and co-operatives have been conceived, along with the panchayat system, as major instruments for bringing about social and economic justice.

But despite these, the divide between the two Indias grows. This is partly because the efforts made by the government have by and large been ineffective. Laws have been enacted but rarely implemented. Policies have remained on paper, as a collection of pious intentions, without workable action plans. The few programmes that have been implemented have rarely reached the intended beneficiaries, especially in the manner required. Reservations, representations and various fiscal benefits have either been fraudulently diverted to ineligible individuals, or have been restricted to very narrow élites of the economically weaker and minority communities. These élites, even as they benefit from the power and dispensation meant for their communities, are alienated from the latter and co-opted into the first India, the India of the rich and the powerful.

The same élites have by and large dominated co-operative, panchayat and other local institutions, including the elected ones.

In fact, if anything, many of these efforts have served to further polarize society. There have been anti-reservation riots across the country and great resentment at what has been perceived as a pampering of the minorities. All this would not matter if the measures had actually reached the poor, the weak and the minorities, and strengthened them. As this has not happened, the resultant polarization has left them even more vulnerable than before.

Clearly, a new strategy is required.

Defusing Social Tension and Violence

In the last two decades, India has been rocked by social upheavals based not only on the historical communal issue, but around various other issues of social and economic justice. To list just a few: terrorism in Punjab, Assam and the various North-Eastern states; the Jharkhand agitation; social unrest in Kashmir; violence in many other parts of the country on questions of reservation for backward classes, language, environmental destruction, political corruption and regional disparities; and, above all, violence between social classes, between the landed and the landless, the upper castes and the Dalits, the 'developers' and the displaced tribals. Though these social turmoils can be seen as a manifestation of the growing awareness among the people of their rights, the tragedy is that our social and political institutions and the government seem incapable of handling this growing awareness and of channelizing the energy that it releases into constructive rather than restive social processes.

The Genesis of Social Protests

Social and economic oppression has always invoked social protest, and hopefully will always continue to do so.

Social protests are, therefore, an inherent part of any society and history has shown that the absence of social protest in a society can at best be a temporary phenomenon, usually as a result of extreme oppression.

Before the advent of democracy, and of the press and mass media, social protests were perhaps the only way in which the rulers of a State could be made to understand the true feelings of the people. Such social protests were reflected, initially, in the writings of poets and writers. Even in conditions of extreme oppression, when the mere verbalizing of protests was prohibited, human ingenuity discovered ways of expressing protest. The underground 'gutter poets' of pre-revolution France, the curfew songs of the military controlled Mizoram of the late Sixties, or the blank new columns during the days of the Emergency and censorship, all bear testimony to this. Gandhi, through his 'satyagraha' and the Civil Disobedience Movement, gave greater conceptual clarity to the notion of social protest, and also established its moral legitimacy and effectiveness as a means of social change.

Any history of social transformation would show that it is not bureaucracies, plans, committees or seminars that have brought about social change; it has always been people's protests and movements, led and supported by those who refused to accept things as they were, always aspiring for a better world. In recent years, both in the former USSR and Eastern Europe and in a large number of Third World societies, some of these movements have been spearheaded from within the system, no doubt as a reflection of the feelings of a people too terrorized to speak out openly.

Therefore, the fact that the Indian people are, collectively and individually, protesting about something or the other all the time is not the worrying thing. What is worrying is that we, as a society, are not responding to the protests within, are not able to learn from them, and are not allowing the energies inherent in them to facilitate the process of social transformation and are, in fact, very often, allowing vested interests to either exterminate or co-opt and corrupt them.

The most deep-rooted protests in any society are those born out of a threat to the cultural and social identity of a people. History has shown that even the most timid of communities, who might only mildly protest against economic oppression, rise up in arms if their cultural identity is threatened. For this identity is primordial and the basis of their own sense of belonging.

The tendency to impose centralized, insensitive and inappropriate decisions on the people of India 'in the public interest' has been another source of social tension. The protests of groups and communities, of tribals, the rural and urban poor, and women, have been increasingly ignored on the plea that their sacrifices are required in the 'national interest', or the interest of the majority. Millions of people have been displaced by various government activities, on the justification that their displacement would benefit the nation. Rural communities have been deprived of their forests, their grazing lands, even their water, on the plea that the majority, 'the nation', needs them. Whole strata of society are being denied even the basic resources for survival, for these resources are required by the 'nation', 'in the public interest', to build cities, and hotels, and cars, and luxury houses.

The ability of the State to appropriate resources and suspend rights of communities 'in the public interest', is dependent on its credibility with the people. If the State is genuinely seen as just, using national resources most efficiently and equitably, then the communities might be willing to put up with their own deprivations. After all, they have been putting up with them for so many decades. But the State is progressively being seen as an agent of the powerful, of the oppressors, of rich India. Forests, to which villagers with traditional rights are denied access, because they are required 'in the national interest' to preserve the ecological balance, are overnight cut for contractors who transform them into veneer and furniture for the rich. Water, which is denied to parched agricultural fields, or to rural areas for drinking or sanitation, is diverted to cities in the 'public interest', and then flushed down toilets at the rate of twelve litres per flushing. A poor farmer is denied a loan to replace his old, almost useless plough, for the money is required, 'in the public interest', to give loans to buy cars in the city. The irony of the situation was brought out very aptly in a court case some years back, when a state government tried to justify its order to clear a city of pavement and *jhuggi jhonpri* dwellers by arguing that this was necessary in the interests of the 'citizens of that city'. However, it turned out that these *jhuggi jhonpri* and pavement dwellers constituted more than 50 per cent of the city's population. Who, then, were the real citizens of that city, and what was in their interest?

A State which becomes deaf to the individual and collective voices of its thousands of 'minority' communities, groups and social segments who collectively form an overwhelming majority of the people, is forcing these voices to become increasingly strident and to replace protest with aggression and aggression with violence. A State which no longer listens to what its poets, its writers, its film-makers are saying, has lost its sensitivity and thereby its moral right to govern.

Ethnic Security

The tendency of individuals and groups to close ranks and identify themselves with their most immediate fraternities is aggravated when these individuals and groups feel threatened. Isolated communities and ideologies always end up being more fundamentalist.

If minority (or, for that matter, the majority) groups in this country are to be weaned away from the influence of fundamentalism, they must be made to feel socially and economically secure. Their culture and religion must be protected from external violence and from unnecessary moralizing. It must be recognized that social transformation can only legitimately come from within a society or community. This is as true for India as a whole, where we must resist international pressures to conform to their perceptions of propriety, as it is for specific communities and sub-groups. External threats to the identity of such communities only strengthen the traditionalists and fundamentalists within them, and marginalize the progressive forces. While supporting those objective conditions which are progressive, external pressures and threats must never be used to try and achieve social transformation. These are invariably counterproductive and, in the long run, much more time is saved if the internal processes of change, which exist within all social groups, are allowed to blossom and strengthen without being snuffed out by inappropriate external interventions.

Social Protest and Violence

A contrast with earlier decades shows the marked increase in levels of violence that social protests have begun to manifest. The time lag between the beginning of a protest and its becoming violent has also shrunk to a point where many of these 'movements' are violent almost from the start.

The violence manifested in such movements often comes out of the growing belief that the State only responds and takes notice when protests become violent, that it only listens to big bangs, hardly ever to grievances that are routed through institutions. Unfortunately, recent history supports this belief. There have been few cases where the government has shown sensitivity to popular, non-violent movements, while it has bent over backwards to accommodate even the unjustified demands of strident and violent movements, even when they have little popular base. There could hardly be a better way of promoting social violence in the country, and of brutalizing a society to a point where historical traditions of debate and consensus are lost for ever.

The weakening of social and political institutions and the brutalization of the state agencies and the society, have left the government with very few options. The government's inability to arrest social and economic oppression and contain the tendency for religious and cultural hegemony is matched by its inability to anticipate social discontent and unrest and to defuse it. The progressive elements in any community, who would ordinarily have internally contained the discontent, and spoken on behalf of the community to the government and to elected representatives, have long been marginalized. Their past inabilities to make the government see reason, and in some cases even their betrayal by the government, have made them ineffective. Politicians, administrators and community leaders have mostly lost their public credibility, or have become disillusioned and therefore unwilling to act as social mediators. In such a situation there is nothing to stand between the people and violence.

Clearly, a new strategy is required as also an identification of the major tasks that lie ahead.

The Major Tasks

To Strengthen the Weakest Segments of Our Society

History has shown very clearly that one cannot constructively transform a society from the outside. All genuine social transformations have been initiated from within the society, even though in many cases the genesis for such transformation lay in the cross-fertilization of ideas and experiences from different societies.

Right to Work: The ability of a society or community to transform itself from within is dependent on various factors, some of which can be significantly influenced from the outside. For one, a social group or community which does not have basic economic security is not likely to have the strength to fight for social change, for invariably the very same vested interests also control their immediate economic destinies. Therefore, a first precondition is an assured right to economic security, through an unconditional right to work. The requirement for a home, a liveable natural environment and basic physical security are also fundamental to economic security. Therefore, along with a right to work, these people must also be provided a right to housing, a right to a liveable environment and a right to basic protection under the law. Job reservations in the government or for political office at higher levels, while important in altering the power structure in the long term, by and large benefit urban metropolitan populations or those who can move to urban areas. However, most of those requiring help live in the rural areas. Therefore, some other strategy has to be adopted for them. Appropriate jobs have to be created in rural areas. These jobs must draw upon the traditional skills of the rural people and must be self-sustaining after a while, for otherwise they will soon be diverted to the stronger sections of society. The two obvious answers are to generate employment by strengthening traditional artisanal and handicraft activities, and by involving the people in the protection and regeneration of the environment. Very little investment would be required for implementing this strategy, as opposed to any other.

Right to Education: But in order to ensure that such rights, once given, actually benefit those for whom they are designed, it is essential that economically backward communities be provided universal basic education. In some ways this is far more important than mere reservation for government jobs (for which too educational attainments are a prerequisite). It seems that almost the only way of empowering these communities and social groups to transform themselves and their position in the larger social structure, is by enhancing their abilities to comprehend the prevailing social and economic processes, to articulate their own perceptions, experiences and demands, and to manoeuvre effectively in the prevailing political ethos. An important, perhaps the most important, instrumentality for this is literacy and education. The State must, therefore, not only ensure that an adequate number of (functional) schools are provided for children belonging to the economically weaker communities, but based on an assessment of the actual situation, provide the required economic incentives to ensure that these children actually go to those schools.

Of particular importance is the need to provide incentives to ensure that every girl child can attend school, so that it becomes economically advantageous for parents to send girls to school rather than to keep them at home or make them work. A justification for providing special allocations for educating the economically backward segments of society, and among them giving incentives to the girl child, is provided by statistics on national literacy which establish that literacy rates of the SC/ST are less than half those of other sections of society. Similarly, literacy rates among women are about a half of that of males, and of SC/ST women a third of other women. On the other hand, more literacy among girls can act as a spur to greater literacy among boys too, whereas the opposite is not true.

Nutrition and Health Care: The education imparted in schools must be supplemented by a basic nutrition package, through schemes like the midday meal scheme started in Tamil Nadu, as well as an adequate package of health care for children. This would not only be an added incentive for the children to go to school but would also ensure that they have at least the basic nutritional level required to assimilate the learning with which the school will provide them.

To Restore and Strengthen Socio-Political Processes

One major reason for the non-resolution and even strengthening of the major social contradictions in India has been the increasing techno-managerial nature of State intervention and governance. Social and political problems have repeatedly been perceived as techno-managerial ones and are therefore unsuccessfully tackled through technological and managerial initiatives. Poverty and hunger have been treated as problems arising primarily out of low productivity, rather than from distortions in our social and economic structure. Social oppression and injustice have been addressed by setting up various bureaucratic institutions, commissions, committees, and through the enactment of laws and the appointment of judges, rather than through a process of mass socialization and education. At the same time even acknowledged socio-economic issues have been reduced only to economic issues, where solutions are being prescribed. We therefore have a situation today where economic growth and productivity are unable to ensure a corresponding decrease in poverty and hunger, and where a collection of progressive laws and benign policies are unable to ensure equity and justice. The 'social delivery system' is not able to meet the challenge of distributive justice.

Much of this is due to the overshadowing of socio-political processes by the techno-managerial ones. The techno-managerial culture has grown phenomenally since independence, cornering much of available human talent and even prevailing over the historically dominant administrative culture of the government. To become technologists, managers or techno-managerial administrators has become the primary ambition of the Indian educated classes. Very few want to be school teachers, or social workers, or to join the 'dirty world' of politics, let alone joining the inherently long term battles waged by those interested in structural change on behalf of the Dalits, the tribals, the women and child labour. And the social system dominated by these techno-managers has ensured that these preferred professions become the most lucrative and among the most powerful.

What is most worrying is the infiltration of techno-managerial influences into the portals of administration. The modern administrator is increasingly seeing himself or herself as 'managing' a district or a department, which has been depopulated of human beings and human issues and problems, and converted into a 'corporation' comprised of data-bases and a collection of statistics, preferably computerized and subjected to modern systems analyses. The choice of solutions are dictated by the 'software' available and problems are identified and 'solved' on computer screens.

Historically, the major strength of the administrators has been their ability to keep in touch with the people and to understand the objective reality better and more richly by drawing general principles from a host of individual interactions, through intuitive induction. Some of the most perceptive accounts of societies and social processes in India have come from administrators who had honed their abilities to deal with grassroots understanding and spent much of their time and energy in going round and seeing and understanding for themselves the ground reality. In the process they also developed the ability to directly intervene in social processes in a sensitive yet effective manner. Unfortunately, much of this is being lost today not, as is sometimes argued, because the workload of administrators has increased but because the priorities have changed and their method of functioning has become increasingly managerial.

Inherent to a techno-managerial culture are the concepts of centralization, of mega-projects and of 'hi-tech'. These are seen as efficient, utilizing 'economies of scale' and subject to easier monitoring and control. But efficiency and benefits are measured purely in economic terms, without any reference to the values of equity or human welfare. Monitoring and control is done solely with economic objectives in mind. Forests, water, soil, housing, education and health are all understood in purely financial terms whereas the social, cultural, human and even ecological 'costs and benefits' are being labelled 'intangible' and therefore beyond the comprehension of the techno-managers. Planning and development emanating from such a basis can never serve human welfare, which itself would be labelled intangible and therefore incalculable and irrelevant.

In the non-economic areas of governance, social movements and protests and criticism of the government are seen as deviant behaviour of maladjusted social elements. There is a contempt for social and political processes which are seen as impediments to 'economic growth'. National objectives are tautologically defined to be identical to what is the prevalent fashion among the techno-managers, whether it be moving to the twenty-first century or emerging as a regional and even a world power. Strategies of development are also accordingly formulated, whether they be through technology missions or through government-sponsored and well-behaved voluntary bodies. There is no scope for dissent, no possible difference of opinion and certainly no other acknowledged way of dealing with any problem anywhere, apart from the one prescribed from the top.

There is an urgent need to change this. The predominant culture of the State and the government has to be socio-political, and technology and management must subserve this culture. Economic development, unless it subserves the objective of equity, will only worsen the divide between the rich and the poor. Technology which is not appropriate to our society and environment will only impoverish the nation. And administration which has forgotten the individual and the community will only exacerbate social tensions. A polity which denies its basic political identity will be doomed to failure.

To Decentralize Power and Control

We see, in India today, a large divide between the privileged and the oppressed—what has earlier been called the phenomenon of the two Indias. This divide manifests itself along urban and rural lines, but also within urban and rural areas. There are the few who, because of historical reasons, have positions of power and influence. They control much of India's resources and use them in perpetuation of their interest.

Efforts since independence to either narrow or diffuse this divide have had little success. This is perhaps due to the strategy adopted, which assumed that this divide, at least at the time of independence, was based on caste lines and along the urban-rural dimension. Efforts were, therefore, made to involve the historically oppressed castes and other rural people in processes of representation and governance. It was also recognized that various other groups like women, tribals and minority communities had been neglected as well and efforts were made to include them in the mainstream of decision-making. The Community Development Programme and its subsequent incarnation, the panchayati raj, was one manifestation of this. Reservations for scheduled castes and scheduled tribes in panchayat bodies and in the government and educational institutions was another manifestation. Efforts were made to ensure the representation of various historically neglected segments of society in the Parliament, state legislatures and other institutions of government. Social and economic incentives were given, laws were framed and efforts were made to educate and socialize the people of India.

Despite these efforts, the ground reality did not change much. Representatives of historically oppressed communities, as already described, were either co-opted into the system, or remained ineffective due to their inability to manoeuvre among powerful vested interests.

As a reaction to the ineffectiveness of the community development and panchayati raj experiments and partly to the rise of 'vernacular' élites that had emerged from the lower tiers of polity, there started a process of centralization by which decision-making powers were once again taken over by a small group of policy-makers and intellectuals at the Centre. The arguments offered were that the people of India, especially the oppressed and minority communities, were too weak, ignorant, steeped in unscientific traditionality, and stratified and divided among themselves, to plan for their own future and ensure social justice and progress. Such centralization resulted in a perpetuation of the phenomenon of two Indias, different in its superficial manifestations from traditionally divided societies but identical to them in the inherent and fundamental oppression and injustice.

The present divide between those who oppress and those who are oppressed transcends caste structures and the rural-urban divide, and is rooted in a socio-economic order which allows a few to reap the benefits of oppressing the many. Efforts at tackling this divide at any other level, or through other structures, would at best result in a realignment of forces, keeping intact the antagonistic relations between the oppressed and the oppressor.

But then, what is the solution? If, during the last forty years, both decentralized and centralized governance has failed, what options remain?

The new commitment to decentralization of the system (on which there seems to be a consensus emerging across parties) stems from the conviction that it is the only way in which popular participation and a measure of social justice can be achieved. However, the lessons of history cannot be ignored. History establishes that for decentralization to succeed, certain objective conditions are required. Local communities have to be strengthened and socio-political processes regenerated. The fact that decentralization is to be preferred to centralization, whatever its weaknesses, needs to be recognized and the commitment to make decentralization work, however long it takes, needs to be reaffirmed. But decentralization is not merely to be seen as involving local people but of restructuring the very system of governance so that they are not just to be accommodated through some co-optative moves but themselves made to run the show. The process of decentralization is to be made relevant to all aspects of decision-making: to the setting of objectives, to the identification of methodologies, to actual implementation, and above all to the determination of needs and of development priorities. Similarly, decentralized control implies the control of local communities, within broad national parameters, over their physical and natural resources and over the financial resources allocated to them. It also implies administrative control over local level functionaries.

In terms of development objectives, it is recognized that there are certain fundamental objectives which have been accepted by all and are, at least at the present time, unquestionable. These are based on what are seen as absolute social values and include equity and social justice; empathy towards living creatures; access to a minimum standard of living, health, environment and shelter; access to information and education; and a reasonable freedom to pursue preferred social and economic activities. These objectives are taken as given because what a decentralized process does is to effectively work them out—which was not possible under a centralized system of governance.

There are other social objectives which are not based on absolute values and are therefore not necessarily universal to the whole country. These objectives must be determined at the lowest appropriate level, as earlier specified, and not at a national or state level. Furthermore, these are objectives that are better realized by social organizations of the people than by government. In essence, then, *decentralization is to be conceived as not merely devolution of government authority within an existing order known as the State, but also a shift of power from State and government institutions to those of civil society.*

The Weeding Out of Corruption

One of the major impediments in ensuring social justice has been the high and increasing levels of corruption in the government and in political and public institutions. Efforts to reach benefits to the poor, to give them a share of the economic fruits of development and to provide basic educational and health facilities for them have repeatedly been frustrated by huge 'leakages' in the system. Schemes designed for the economic upliftment of the weaker sections of society have given birth to legends of how the money earmarked for the poor was pocketed and how 'the same cow has been distributed again and again' under these and similar schemes. Our public distribution system only reaches a part of those it has been designed for, many of our rural schools do not function, sub-health centres rarely have the medicines that the government has paid for, roads are built only on paper, or never maintained despite the money spent on their supposed maintenance, and many forests are planted without any evidence of the consequent trees. These are some of the well-documented parameters of 'leakages' in the process of reaching development benefits to the poor.

On the other hand, there are huge illegal processes of appropriation under way which are rapidly diverting and depleting common and public resources, especially those in rural areas. Illegal forest extraction is well known, as is organized encroachment of government and public lands, often with the connivance of officials. Lesser known appropriations involve the rampant theft of electricity, which is officially recorded as transmission losses and amounts to 25 per cent of the country's power generation, illegal diversion of streams and rivers for industry at the cost of villages and local communities, illegal and ecologically destructive mining, shady land deals where public, common and forest land is sold to the rich for luxury housing or for élite recreational projects, and appropriation of scarce raw materials like cement, steel, cotton and fertilizers.

The third dimension of corruption involves the evasion of taxes, duties, tariffs and other dues to the government exchequer. This in itself is rampant, and is supported by a host of professionals who build their careers and fortunes by assisting individuals and corporations in breaking and 'getting around' the law. These three forms of corruption have given birth to a whole new economy often referred to as the 'parallel' or 'black' economy, which has sometimes been calculated to be as large as, if not larger than, the 'white' economy.

We consequently have a state which is crippled by corruption, unable to protect common and scarce resources from illegal appropriation, unable to collect its dues from the rich and powerful and unable to deliver even the small percentage of its remaining meagre resources to the poor, who desperately need them.

Unfortunately, corruption does not restrict itself to just these aspects. It contaminates almost all aspects of governance. Governmental agencies responsible for ensuring justice, peace, law and order have also been corrupted. Justice can be bought and sold. Those with money and influence can endlessly harass those without, and can unleash a reign of terror which is reminiscent of the Mafia. All the sections of society are breeding criminalized sub-cultures whose power is based on the strength of money and political patronage. Political and social institutions have themselves got corrupted and it has become more or less a truism that wherever there is power or money, there is bound to be corruption.

The State has, in its own manner, acknowledged and assimilated this culture of corruption. The elaborate structure of government and financial rules and rules of conduct for government officials, the audit, anti-corruption and vigilance mechanisms, the creation of Lokayukts and Lokpals, some of the rationale for the Anti-defection Bill, and the admitted difficulties in reliably identifying those segments of the society that are economically backward, are manifestations of the State's acknowledgement of the prevailing culture of corruption. The regrettable decision to liberalize controls and laws concerning the recovery of dues, the giving of frequent amnesties to tax evaders, and the unfortunate decision to reward officials, for example from the customs, with a percentage of the value of goods seized by them, are the beginnings of a process by which the culture of corruption is assimilated and given a legitimacy.

But just as there is a 'parallel economy' emanating out of economic corruption, so also is there a parallel culture of corruption interfacing with that of the government. To hoard essential commodities, to live opulently much beyond one's legal means of income, to be a tax evader or a smuggler or blackmarketeer, are no longer considered by society to be reprehensible. Elaborate rationalizations have been formulated to give social respectability to such activities, so much so, that having a tax raid is today considered, in certain sections of society, a mark of having arrived into the select group of the economically successful.

Added to this there is the inevitable corruption of our social institutions, even of the most sacrosanct of them, the nuclear family. Harassment, dowry deaths and bride burning are some of the more horrific manifestations of a corrupted culture where even the most fundamental human relationships have been reduced to commercial transactions, and basic human empathy has been totally lost.

There are many reasons for this growth in corruption. First, the government and corporate sector have unleashed on the citizens a culture of consumerism, where new commodities are daily entering the markets and tempting the consumer to join the rat race and buy and consume far more than he or she needs or can afford. The consolidation of the consumerist culture has been ably supported by the mass media, printed and electronic, mostly at public expense. The consumption of commodities, in excess of real needs, has been powerfully promoted through advertising, marketing and packaging, in recent times increasingly aimed at children. Junk foods are being promoted, despite conclusive evidence from other countries of the disastrous impact these have on the eating habits and nutritional levels, especially of the young. Elaborate packaging, including tetrapacks, are being encouraged despite their being environmentally destructive. And much of this damage is being promoted through 'official' electronic media and through newspapers and magazines which get subsidized newsprint and other inputs. Scarce resources like power, petroleum products, steel, cement, chemicals and minerals, wood, paper and water are being diverted to the production of these consumer goods, at the cost of basic sectors. Valuable foreign exchange is also being frittered away.

Acquisition of consumer goods, whether they be the latest model of car, video, TV, stereo, or fancy suits and kitchenware, including microwave ovens, has become a national preoccupation, of late promoted as a matter of policy, as has happened with the most recent relaxation of baggage rules for Indians returning from abroad. Increasingly, urban markets are flooded with more and more luxury goods. Even village communities are not immune to this and evidence exists to show that in many of the rural households where money is not available for basic necessities, an increasing proportion of household expenditure is being diverted to the purchase of luxury items.

The internal and peer group pressures to acquire commodities can never be fully satisfied, except perhaps by the very rich. However, for the various middle classes the prospects of rapid increases in income are not high, especially in the sort of economy that operates in India which hits the fixed and salaried income groups the hardest. Perhaps the more fatalistic pin their hopes on various lotteries that have become the new opiate of the masses, but most turn to corruption for satisfying their increasing demands. It seems rational that a government wanting to curb the culture of corruption would first take steps to curb the culture of consumerism, or at least to withdraw the prevalent official sponsorship to it. But there is no sign of this. If anything, with the growing emphasis on 'integration into the world economy' the global culture of consumerism is being brought to the doorstep.

The second basis for the culture of corruption is provided by our education system which is increasingly producing what can best be described as 'primarily economic creatures'. Recent student demonstrations against reservations for backward classes manifested their contempt for 'lower' jobs like pulling rickshaws and selling vegetables, and revealed the growing élite's perceptions of different occupations and the consciousness of a 'hierarchy' among jobs. The most distressing aspect of the whole matter was that the student community, by and large, did not even realize the insulting implications of their methods of protest on the majority of India's population, which is aspiring for those very occupations that the students dismissed with such great contempt. Meanwhile the 'yuppie culture' spread by the mass media is permeating the minds of middle class, university-educated youth.

With the erosion of traditional, religious and social values, many of which were in any case outdated and inappropriate, the role of education and educational institutions in providing an alternate set of values has become crucial. However, our educational system is among the most neglected aspects of state activity. Despite the multiple, perhaps paramount, demands being made on the system, our investment in it has never exceeded a meagre level. And whatever is being invested is diverted to either directly corrupt uses or in spreading crassly utilitarian values which end up in breeding vulgar economism—and anxiety on that count—among our young.

Both a curbing of consumerism and a revamping of the educational system are essential if corruption has to be weeded out of Indian society and relegated to its historical position of being a deviant phenomenon rather than the all pervasive culture that it has become today. However, some immediate measures are also required to curb the further growth of the already very high levels of corruption, and to create the sort of objective conditions within which the prevailing trend of social legitimization of corruption is checked. Such a trend, if it were to grow and consolidate, would undermine all future efforts at fighting this social menace, for the corrupt would support each other and their culture.

Right to Information: The first immediate step required for curbing the growing levels of corruption in our society is an assured access to information. At present, there is no implementable legal or constitutional right to information for the citizens of India. Just as the culture of secrecy makes it impossible to get even the most harmless piece of information out of a bureaucracy, so the plea of patents and trade secrets, along with no legal compulsions to divulge any information, makes even corporate information inaccessible. In this environment of secrecy, all sorts of skulduggery flourish.

To supplement the right to information, there has to be a strengthening of those processes by which government officials and other functionaries are made answerable for their actions and inactions. The healthy administrative tradition of 'fixing responsibility' must be revived and even committees must be made answerable and, if necessary, prosecutable, for any dubious collective decisions. All functionaries must be persuaded out of the comfortable stance they have adopted, i.e., as long as they are not personally corrupt, the responsibility of checking corruption among their subordinates and in their departments is not theirs. Such an attitude should be treated as a 'sin of omission' and accordingly punished. Unless all the major institutions of the State—from the executive to the judiciary to the political parties to public corporations—and the beneficiaries of their patronage—from educational institutions to NGOs and the mass media—are willing to take a tough stand on this issue, and to open their functioning to critical public scrutiny, the spectre of corruption will only grow larger. And the more it grows, the less will there be any chance to deal with poverty, either through governmental policies or, what is more basic, through empowering the poor themselves. Indeed, the worst form of *disempowerment* is the growth and persistence of corruption in public life. For, quite apart from corruption being a form of victimization, the poor too get afflicted by it and are in the process rendered impotent.

Ethical Imperatives

Beyond the institutional steps needed to restructure the processes of power and root out its worst pathologies like endemic corruption and criminalization, there is a need to enlist human sensitivity on behalf of the poor at more basic levels. There is a need to go beyond the political, the social and the ecological domains and tap the moral and ethical domain. It is not enough to provide an intellectual profile of an alternative model, or to inject into the dominant intellectual paradigm and the economistic ethic of our time social and ecological considerations. The essential task that faces us is to render the actions of the State and other corporate entities humane, to ensure that the processes generated by 'development' do not destroy diverse cultures and their roots both in nature and in unique human beings in the name of some abstract idea, be it of profit or of some absolutist ideology.

Keeping Hope Alive

Central to such a task is the paramount need of the time we find ourselves in: how to keep *hope* alive. As stated by the leading educationist, Denis Goulet, by a purely rational calculus of future probabilities, the development enterprise of most countries is doomed to fail. The poor can never cope so long as the rich continue to consume wastefully and to devise ideological justifications for the same. In all probability, technological and resource gaps will continue to widen and vast resources will continue to be devoted to destructive armaments. Exacerbated feelings of national sovereignty will, in all likelihood, continue to coexist alongside an ever more urgent need to institute new forms of governance and problem-solving. By any rational scenario projectible over the next fifty years, development will continue to wreak ecological destruction, and it will remain the privilege of a relative few, while underdevelopment will continue to be the lot of the vast majority. Only through a major act of imagination and a new stirring of consciousness can even a candle of hope be generated. The French social critic, Jacques Ellul, writes eloquently of the need for hope in a time of abandonment.

Indeed, it is precisely when it is becoming clear that the present is not sustainable and when realistic projections indicate a dismal scenario for the future, at any rate for the suffering part of humanity, that we need to remind ourselves, based on the totality of human experience, that the future has never been predestined and can be reordained, if only we have the confidence—based on hope—that this is possible. And not just that it is possible but that it is *necessary* and indeed inherent in the scheme of things, and hence incumbent upon us all. As the title of this chapter says, it is an ethical imperative.

Such an imperative cannot be in the form of a disembodied and abstract idea. It must arise out of a certain process of history, of not just being but becoming, emerging out of a collective experience of something that is at once organic and specific, located at once in the mind as in the reality 'out there', evolved over time and hence real yet continuously evoking new definitions of the challenge that lies ahead. Discovering new priorities, particularly on the margins of society, not necessarily through great events as through small signs of ordinary assertion, all of it as part of a larger reawakening and restructuring of civil society.

The First Indian Enterprise

Independent India started with two projects—partly interrelated but in many ways different from each other—viz., the project of building a State and the project of Development, one promising an all-encompassing presence in a plural society, and the other promising a major *economic* (and technological) transformation of a traditional society toward a modernist paradigm helped by education, urbanization, mass media exposure and, in Karl Deutsch, the political scientist's terms, 'social mobilization' through which the mass of the people 'become available for new patterns of socialization and behaviour'.

Conceptually, 'development' was to be a project of the State (this was central to the Nehruvian vision) but as the State had not really come through in any organic sense (encompassing the enormous cultural diversity of the land), development became a project of the élite or rather, a self appointed arm of the élite, viz., the bureaucratic administration which, as it was by its very nature colonial and remote, led to an increasingly exclusivist structure of power. In the process, the State too got reduced into a mere government, a government from one centre—*the* centre with a capital 'C', a colonial and colonizing Centre.

The only way an enduring structure of a State could be built was by drawing into its corpus the various cultural and regional identities that obtained in the socio-political space that it had inherited from colonial administration—and the ethical systems that they embodied—and providing them with a sense of authenticity and a measure of self-governance. Only through such an organic corpus could a humane State have been built. Failing that all you could have was an administration, based on files and procedures, not a State as a moral presence.

The pursuit of a monolithic (hence socially steamrollering and homogenous) model of the State necessarily precluded a diversified and plural approach to 'development', thus leading to the inevitable neglect of (in turn promoting ignorance of and distancing from) the ground realities that were obtained in various cultural and ethical domains. In turn this led to a reflection of abstractions at the top in abstractions at the bottom. Thus the pursuit of 'prosperity' in macro terms of necessity produced 'poverty' in macro terms too—the same scenario of high-rise and hi-tech industrialization alongside malnutrition, ill-health, hunger and starvation deaths. Even the scenario of 'exploitation' and 'marginalization' turned out to be standardized: enforced unemployment, forced evictions from land, forced immigration following destruction of ecologies and the village social nexus, low-paid wages (even below 'minimum wages' which are themselves exploitative), growth of child labour and of prostitution not as a vocation but for sheer physical survival. With all this the scope for culture-specific and ethical responses to deprivation and disparities became marginalized too.

Over time, such a texturing of poverty and disempowerment led, first, to an incredible expansion of the human machine (the bureaucracy) with the ostensible purpose of dealing with 'poverty' defined in standardized patterns and through centrally sponsored schemes. And, then, after it was demonstrated to these bureaucracies that these methods were not working and were ill-suited to remove poverty or reduce disparities, deciding to concentrate on the modern sector and leaving the poor out of the purview of the 'State' (and, without admitting it, out of the purview of the 'Market' too).

Unfortunately, in the meanwhile, the exploited, the deprived and dispossessed and socially uprooted people have also been brainwashed into thinking of themselves in one single *leitmotiv* of being the 'poor', the 'poor wretches', the 'poor things'—being induced to be pitied and patronized. They seem to have lost their capacity to endure and find their own diverse ways of dealing with their reality. Even their 'struggles' are no more than 'demands'.

Is a New Indian Enterprise on the Anvil?

Not quite, fortunately. While I do not want to be misunderstood as romanticizing their plight, I happen to believe that the so-called 'poor' are the true bearers of India's cultural resilience, they are slowly realizing that there is no 'place' for them in this system and will soon arrive at two simultaneous judgements: first, that as there is no justice in the system there is little point in keeping on hoping that something will be 'delivered' by the rich and the powerful; and, second, that this does not mean the end of the world and that they should work out their own path to salvation—they know how to, they are convinced the rich and the powerful do not!

Nor is it just a question of the so-called 'poor' seeking a way out of both the interstices of the State and the tapestries of development. It is also a series of other social groups and communities (and not just the poor among each of them)—the artisans, the farmers, the women, the millions of children and adolescents and the grown-up 'youth', the educated unemployed, many of whom are being forced to take to crime and 'terrorism'. They are all on the one hand feeling exploited and excluded yet on the other hand seeking their own ethical domains which are providing them with their own 'models' for moving along. Of in fact creating 'alternatives' without ever (unlike academic pundits) using that kind of upstart terminology.

The point is that if the State in India has both failed to provide itself with an appropriate structure and in turn created a model of development that is equally disembodied and culturally and ethically adrift, the people of India will soon have to decide to pursue a course quite different to what recent history had laid out for them. And there is no need necessarily to take this as a set-back to the much proclaimed projects of 'nation-building', 'development' and 'democracy'. It could be seen as providing new openings and ethical spaces for creating new ways of dealing with the problems faced by the people. One could almost say: One phase of the Indian enterprise has failed; another is beginning. One is not sure it will make it, but there certainly is something under way that we should try and unravel. (The first statement on my understanding on 'The Indian Enterprise Today' appeared in the American journal *Daedalus* in 1989 and a subsequent, more recent, one entitled 'Restructuring the Indian Enterprise' in the Annual Number of *Seminar* in January 1993.) The imagery of the poor being 'marginalized', dropped out, excluded, forced to 'stew in their own juice', becoming victims of not just discrimination and displacement but also the fact that they are considered dispensable by the ruling class has its own relevance and validity. This makes them targets of pity, analysis, at best compassion, at worst contempt, of being thought of as culturally backward and irrational and lethargic, etc. It is an imagery that the supposedly most empathetic and radical segment of the intelligentsia has promoted. There is need to look at how in fact the poor themselves 'cope' (despite they themselves being prone to accept the imagery).

Two Distinct Enterprises

The point is that we have two quite different perceptions of the poverty situation and the two have produced quite distinct responses. One is the way the 'problem of poverty' has been conceived by professionals coming from the relatively well-off and often richer sections of society (including a whole set of social workers and activists). These have tried to identify, define and analyse the phenomenon of poverty and sought to both 'manage' the same within a given system and tried to 'alleviate' the same through the project of economic development in which needs (presumably limitless) are matched with resources (presumably scarce) and efforts made to improve living conditions within the constraints of the State under which they operate and the interests that the State serves.

Now, while it is increasingly realized that this particular model of 'dealing with' poverty has not worked as was desired, what is not equally realized is that large sections of the poor are poor *because* of development, because they are the victims of the particular model of economic development that was adopted. Severed from their cultural roots, dispossessed of their own resources, drop-outs (forced out) from the very system that was designed to serve them, although designated as 'poor' and accepted as 'target groups' of various development projects they are increasingly being perceived by sections of the ruling class as threats to stability and 'peace'. Treated as pathologies (inherently backward, inert and lazy, lacking motivation, 'merit' and having no work ethic), they are over time considered parasites that are best excluded from that very model of development that had originally been devised for them. The model has since been penetrated by external agents who treat the poor as both a 'resource'—cheap while they last, dispensed with when not needed—and a pretext for turning every deprivation of the poor into an opportunity for the rich. This is found, for instance, with housing where shortages are announced and the builders' lobby moves in, or when nutritional impoverishment is caused by food processing industries.

It seems clear by now that if we were to follow this particular Indian enterprise based on the project of economic development, we would be trapped. And, the poor would be worst affected. Should we be at all concerned with their fate beyond the make-believe of this project or should we allow them to continue to be left to the inexorable logic of the project? In that lies the crucial ethical question. The questions that the poor themselves face are less ethical than political and strategic in terms of their own strategy of dealing with their reality; the ones we, the non-poor, face are ethical. We need to ask ourselves with a certain sense of history: Is poverty as we know it today not basically a modern phenomenon? What, if any, is the link between poverty of the traditional type and modern poverty? While for heuristic purposes and for holding out warnings and signals, comparison with the older reality or even tracing some of today's indicators of inequity and deprivation to the older reality may be worth exploring, is not the phenomenon that is unfolding before our eyes—a phenomenon that links the local, the national and the global—one of contemporary making and is it not likely (if we go about dealing with it the way we have so far) to endure in the future, indeed get worse? Given the fact that the development model that we have adopted has led to more and more resources and opportunities being available for smaller and smaller sections of the people, can we not visualize a growing interest in sustaining poverty and not just neglecting it but actually using it for perpetuating and enhancing the parasitic lifestyles of both Indians and non-Indians through an 'integration' of the Indian economy into the 'world market'? Is there not there then a critical need to devise new strategies (beyond the usual ones of lobbying in the corridors of power and the Planning Commission) of resistance aimed at the reversal of present reality?

We seem to have arrived at a moment in history in which positioning ourselves *vis-à-vis* the poor has increasingly meant that leaving them out of the purview of the State and the development process is not only considered both economically and politically necessary but also legitimate, given the growing perception that in the modern and post-modern paradigm of the world and 'world order' they are proving to be a drag and an obstacle, a 'noise factor' like an unwanted relation. If one takes the role of the State in such a world, one moves from a liberating and empowering one to a repressive and dominating one, and if the role of capitalism and its relations of production, it is from one of functional exploitation in which the poor and the working class were considered necessary to the economy to one in which the latter are seen as sources of growing demands and conflicts and violence that one moves. Hence substitutes are imperative. Even the 'movements' waged in the name of the poor—and the various development NGOs—seem to on the whole leave out the real poor, not necessarily out of design or deceit (though this too cannot be ruled out in all cases) but because there is no larger and comprehensive ethical movement any more, that is coherent and capable of mobilizing diverse social and political constituencies on the basis of being rooted in civil society.

The Other Indian Enterprise

That takes us to the other Indian enterprise that I spoke of earlier. While some of us still continue to feel concerned about the burning issues of our time—including poverty, the root of them all—and may feel ethically driven to effectively intervene in the moment of history that was spoken of above, it is increasingly becoming clear that if we are to prove relevant or, rather, not become irrelevant and filled with a sense of despair devoid of 'hope', we need to see how the poor themselves are thinking of the situation they face. Is it in any way different from the prescriptions held out by planners and developers, is it that over time the poor too have been made to think in the same way, of trying to find a 'place in the system' which means getting merged into the global poverty ghetto? Or is it that the poor are likely to become the main instrument of creating an alternative, both for themselves and hence necessarily—through the various 'struggles' and strategies of sustaining themselves despite everything—for the world around them. Are the strategies of survival (including the struggles), at least some of them, emanating from the victims of the system, the State and the global establishment as against those devised by the latter? Increasingly, the poor (when not fully marginalized and excluded) are being imposed upon and taken for a ride both by their exploiters and by their liberators (not just the do-gooders but even the 'revolutionaries'). What then is the enterprise in which the poor themselves, with their diverse political, social and spatial networks, are found? After all, let us face it, they have survived for a long time. And are not exactly being liquidated (except for some of them). Why? How have they managed?

Any attempt to answer this question must go beyond mere recipes or formulae for 'dealing with' poverty, 'managing' it or even 'countering' present structures which are all of course involved in moving towards both a new understanding and a new enterprise based on a new interpretation of the unfolding reality, of the nature of the transition that lies ahead. Nor can such an enterprise be exclusively focusing on poverty in any narrow economistic sense, leaving out all other considerations that are pressing for attention. It is only the rich who have both an exclusive and an excluding mind-set. Not the poor, who must of necessity relate to the whole and try to transform the whole for then only can things change.

Lastly, such an enterprise must begin with a degree of hope rather than in despair.

As we look at the whole matter within an overall sense of the historical process within the specific Indian setting of today, we find that there are two possible interpretations of 'India-in-transition' and two different strategies of intervening in its evolving future. According to one, the India one knew is in a shambles, a tottering subcontinent, ill at ease with other states and nations on its peripheries, internally disintegrating both territorially and socially, unable to 'hold' politically. Culturally too, even as a civilization—which most people think will somehow survive, weathered as it has so many onslaughts—it is being subjected to multiple pressures that could well upset its traditional balance and staying power. Consumerism and globalization, on the one hand, and the internal tearing apart of its social fabric under the rising cult of violence unleashed by multiple confrontations, on the other. The India that we know is then not just in 'crisis'; it is entering a terminal phase.

But there is quite another way of interpreting the transition, namely, that a new India is struggling to be born. It will be an India that is more complex and both multilayered and multifaceted, not amenable to neat and confident portrayal perhaps. But this may well be because of our failure intellectually to grasp, and socially to come to terms with and accept, a different kind of reality, bearing the impact of the rise of the poor and the unorganized peripheries, having been so long used to looking at the country from the apex and all along looking for 'order' and 'orderly change'. This view is held by not just national politicians and bureaucrats and planners but academic and media dons too, and even social workers and activists occupying various NGO citadels from where so much social change is being engineered.

Discomfort in the Old Order

There has been so much bemoaning by each of these high towers of public 'concern'. We are told that no one obeys the law, long accepted public norms are continuously violated, there has been a great decline in moral standards, everyone seems to be flouting the basic framework of values and commitments enshrined in the 'Constitution'. And yet, could this be because the issues people have to face and grapple with are fundamentally different from the ones they faced and dealt with even ten or fifteen years ago? Are they not caught in a twilight zone, where one moral code is no longer found relevant and a new code is yet to be born? The bemoaning comes from the élite that is too tied to a value system—and an 'order'—that has lost its meaning for a majority of the people.

Underlying such anxiety lies the end of our self confidence as a nation, till recently governed by an identifiable set of people—centrists and nationalists all of them—and according to set norms and predictable ways, in a world that appeared stable and was sustaining 'growth' and 'development' and the nation state.

We also face an end of not just confidence but hope as well, of a chance for most people to make it in life (almost for everyone, except for the very down and out who are excluded and for whom few care anyway; but even for them, there was 'hope' that the development paradigm would one day give scope for them). Of belonging to a nation that was somehow holding. Of minimum conditions of health and education and well-being, with all the indices showing up—life expectancy, decline in infant mortality, crossing the poverty line, stable prices, even literacy, slow as the upswing was, growth of cities which, with all their squalor and emptiness, still gave one a 'chance', the slow improvement in the condition of the 'weaker sections', oppressed no doubt yet fighting for their 'rights'. Much of this is still there and even growing but without that basic *élan* and confidence of it all being in one piece, together transforming the Indian landscape, and not falling apart. That coherence and confidence is no longer there.

This is particularly the case among the 'upwardly mobile' middle class professionals, not just the lawyers and the doctors and the corrupt Public Works Department (PWD) engineers but also the University academics and the journalists and the NGO types and those who have access to either foreign jobs or foreign jaunts *ad nauseum*. But then, even in this hitherto upwardly mobile class there has started taking place a downward mobility, with the spectres of unemployment, inflation, high costs of luxury items like petrol and housing and decline of various services like education and health haunting them, unsettling their long held assumptions about progress and the good life.

With this decline in the earlier confidence about the 'system' and optimism about one's life chances, there is taking place a growing questioning of the ability of the State to deliver the goods, and alongside an erosion of identities—national identity in particular but also a variety of institutional, professional and other secondary identities.

New Strivings, New Sensibility

Instead, there is a search for new identities, new relationships across existing identities, a new understanding of emerging shifts in relationships. The majority is still unsure of the new understandings, because of so much bickering and insecurity, and an almost total lack of new leadership and even more of a new vision, but it is still showing signs of some new *sense* and *sensibility*, a sense of becoming free of older constraints, though no doubt anxious about new constraints that may emerge and unsettle existing arrangements, including possible erosion and even chaos. A growing combination of both a sense of liberation from the old and fear of the new: the typical 'fear of freedom', yet also the possibility of 'freedom from fear', fear that so far held back so many from exploring so much.

For a majority of the people the future seems uncertain and it seems futile to project either a pessimistic or an optimistic sense about it. There is a mood of deep ambivalence on the part of all—left or right, religious or 'secular', traditional or Westernized. While not new for the Indian personality (on which more soon), the new ambivalence presents itself in a drastically changed social and political setting. Also, while there is a growing sense that institutions are no longer operating according to expectations, there seem to be basic differences on how to take it all. For the many who think things are falling apart, there are many others who see value in that happening. After all there isn't much for them in the way things are !

This is particularly the case in urban areas, especially in the larger cities. We have not yet realized the real import of the fast growing numbers of those living in the cities, of the fact that it is from here that the growing turbulence among the poor will find new outlets and completely new types of community and new expressions of social diversity are likely to emerge in these cities that are on so many indicators 'post-modern nightmares'.

Our long neglect of the urban in a period of still greater neglect of rural areas and the environment which is forcing the active population to migrate to the cities is going to force on our attention a completely different set of issues that one did not ordinarily associate with urbanization.

New configurations of caste and community identities will take shape, both within the large and growing backwaters of the 'unorganized sector' and the increasing presence within the migrant communities of the backwards, the Dalits, the socially uprooted and increasingly defiant hordes of women and the literally millions of homeless children selling their labour and their bodies while at the same time defying conventional norms and experimenting with a new set of ideas and behaviour patterns.

As the contours of the new norms and patterns of behaviour are not clear, and as the new actors in the new social and spatial arenas—the young, the women employed from the poorer classes, traditional artisans and 'artists' finding wholly new openings—have no models to fall back on except the continuing hold of caste and family, and as religious beliefs will prove less and less useful in facing the new challenges, we are likely to encounter wholly new contexts given to economic life and new structures provided for secular politics and the composition of civil society.

The 'Mandal phenomenon' has far more to it than mere job reservations or economic threats to the middle class. It signifies the political and social assertion of the poor at a time when both the economic policy of liberalization and the social challenge of 'Hindutva' are threatening their very survival. Needless to say, the India of today has little to offer to this new configuration of social forces which is bound to ask for a new definition of both secular identity and the democratic process.

The Poor and the Young

It was Indira Gandhi who had said that the two majorities of India were the poor and the young. While the claims of the poor as such are increasingly pushed aside and the moral sensitivity of middle classes have suffered erosion, when the majority of the poor happen to be young—growing young with every decade— they become a force to reckon with, even if their growing assertions tend to be increasingly turbulent and unsettling for established structures. In any case, for any appraisal of the future to be adequate, it must take full account of the younger generation, its motifs and cultural contours, its internal composition—with respect to both class and community—and the various cross-currents to which it is likely to be subjected.

It is here that one finds a scenario of intense tension and conflict within this generation. On the one hand one is likely to witness a growing appeal of yuppie style consumerism, drugs and the rise of wayward peer groups beyond families and 'homes', given to new thresholds of crime aimed at greater and greater acquisition of material goods or displays of power through street vandalism and violence against one community or another or against oneself (as with self immolations). On the other hand, the poor among the young are also prone to be swayed by the enticements of the market and the mass media but are more likely to seek this out by occupying spaces within the system even if this means being 'children of the street' or offering themselves as child labour.

As the system is not likely to open out to them and as it is in any case going to be shrinking (less jobs, more jealousies and suspicions), out of the very failure of the project to get integrated into an external colonizing force may emerge a new regeneration, a new identity or at least an active search for one. There may also emerge a new coalition of interests, both drawing on emerging 'movements' of class and ethnicity, and fashioning new ones based on a new hunger for 'education', apprenticeship and experimentation. Perhaps the existing liberal paradigm will prove unable to respond to their strivings and they may discover new styles of fulfilling their own search for 'more democracy'.

It is against this backdrop of the emerging interface of class, youth, gender and ethnicity that the real challenge of restructuring the Indian enterprise will be faced in the years and decades to come. As the State is found more and more to be abdicating its role in ensuring justice and providing social minima of welfare (even in things like education and health, housing and basic amenities), new institutional models will be needed, new self-help collectives in the form of a new genre of cooperatives and 'workers' control' devised (the Kamani experiment providing only one among many models), leading to new structuring of the spaces provided by civil society which were till now dominated by a centralized State and a colonial bureaucracy but which are now likely to get a new lease of life, a new 'liberation'.

Rise of New Politics, New Identity

From this may well emerge a new and different political structure too. There is already under way an incremental withdrawal from New Delhi on the part of not just movements of ethnic identity and regional self-determination but also those of social and economic justice. Be it Mandalism or tribal struggles against displacement and forced evictions; or, the completely new kinds of assertions of feminine personality (deeply ingrained in the revolts against indigenous structures of oppression) than found in the struggles of metropolitan and global-oriented feminists (the latter no doubt opening up spaces for the former); or, the reassertion of 'Bharat', not as schematized by, the peasant leader from Maharashtra, Sharad Joshi (hardly a beacon for the poor, even the traditional poor) but rather as laid out by a real and genuine search for 'cultural democracy' in the yearnings of traditional artisan communities struggling against urban and 'global' tycoons trying to export Indian art and culture, but also of deeply frustrated artists and activists and 'alternate media' exponents seeking a new identity for themselves as well as for the country.

As all this will also militate against the new 'special interests' of professionals and business groups lobbying in the corridors of power and—more pertinently—against new collaborationists with foreign interests masquerading as 'nationalist' politicians (chastising real movements of cultures and nationalities as being 'anti-national'), and as it will also find it difficult to swallow the old socialist rhetoric (which had generated so many expectations which were just let down), a completely new alignment of forces is likely to find fruition.

How does it all sound? At once unsettling for the modernist generation which has lost its moorings and yet opening up new possibilities, new hopes, that may well move the country towards fresh thresholds of democratic self realization. For so many forces that appeared to run helter-skelter that may now get poised to take on new roles and, by so doing, find a new comprehension, a new cohesion. Despite so much uncertainty, so much ambiguity.

One of the continuing cultural traits of the Indian civilization has all along been in terms of its high tolerance of ambiguity. Only the modern hi-tech élite wants to regulate things, 'resolve' contradictions along some rationalist calculus, live by the logic of the excluded middle. The age of these modernists—and their 'post-modern' inheritors—is fast coming to a close, here and elsewhere in the world. This does not mean any return to some pristine past as if such a 'past' were ever there for us to 'revive'. This then is the ambience of a new awakening, a redefinition of Indian identity, one that is at once so uncertain about what lies in store and so pregnant with possibilities. This will call for a series of conceptual efforts—reconstructing national identity, restructuring the 'State', at once decentring and recentring the federal polity. Federating from below, federating regionally (that being the challenge of Punjab and Kashmir and Tamil Nadu) and federating socially (that being the challenge of Mandal), with a deep ecological content (that being the challenge of Narmada) and an extensive economic rationale (that being the challenge of the struggle against globalization), together creating a new and refashioned democratic structure, drawing on fresh convulsions in the social fabric occasioned by new assertions of the poor and the various peripheries.

It is through such a conception of 'a new India (that) is struggling to be born' that we can have some glimpses of a future that could take shape. Hopefully, such a future can be fashioned on the basis of a timely sense of how to respond to a historical reality, and to enable the right actors to so respond. From both the bottoms of the social hierarchy—the poor—and the diverse ethnics and the 'backwards', together announcing a new consolidation of forces.

The Call of the Ethical Imperative

If this be the new enterprise based on a new interpretation of the emerging reality, what should be the role of those among us who till recently held on to the old and yet have for some time now been wanting to become part of the new? It is here that the ethical imperative comes into force: how to at once communicate and commiserate with the new strivings and the new assertions, 'sacrifice' the lifestyles that divide us from them on an almost permanent basis, and do this not just as ecological prudence and the aesthetics of frugality and 'limits' but as ethical choices made out of a sense of sharing and solidarity, of inhabiting a common world which we are together trying to reshape—despite the continuing gaps and cultural distances. The condition of the poor and the cultural correlates of poverty do indeed entail the former but the ethical imperative is essentially based on the latter. By themselves the former exclude class. The latter necessarily includes it. And that is what provides the cutting edge of the politics of poverty. And of the ethics thereof.

Before concluding I should like to make two vital points. First, as was emphasized at the start of 'Reorientating Development', the new enterprise we have in mind is cast in modest and achievable terms—a lot better and different than where we are today but not necessarily aiming at some golden utopia. This is where the practical ontological perspective of the poor must guide us, not the 'perfect state' neurosis of the affluent. As in many other enterprises, here too the best can be the enemy of the good. And to the extent the 'best' is interpreted as 'most' in the sense of more and more consumption of finite resources, it excludes the rights of others because in sheer gratification of what Gandhi called 'greed', it becomes blind to others' needs. Also, those who have sought the best, for themselves or for 'mankind', have, in fact produced a world full of iniquity and exploitation. We should aim at a world of greater equity and less affluence, at an ethic of concern for all instead of an ethic of gratification of individualized selves.

Second, our approach to the ethical imperative is also not cast in abstract philosophical terms but in terms of *active* interventions. And these too not by a select few who alone (like the traditional Brahmins) are supposed to provide ethical directions and guidance to society but by ordinary people—by those who have suffered from the course of secular history so far, have been victims of the historical process. For them the ethical intervention consists in recharting the course of history. If that is aiming high, so be it.

INDEX

Rajni Kothari has written extensively on the interface between governance and human rights, both in a global perspective and in the specific cultural context of the Indian subcontinent. He started the international journal *Alternatives*, founded the Centre for the Study of Developing Societies, and has had a long association with the United Nations University, where he directed the Programme on Peace and Global Transformation. He has been very active in India's human rights movement and was President of the People's Union for Civil Liberties. Rajni Kothari was also the Chairman of the Indian Council of Social Science Research. The most recent position held by him was that of Member of the Planning Commission. He is currently co-chairman of the International Foundation for Development Alternatives (IFDA), Nyon, Switzerland.